Lecture Notes
in Business Information Processing   **326**

More information about this series at http://www.springer.com/series/7911

Sune Dueholm Müller · Jeppe Agger Nielsen (Eds.)

Nordic Contributions in IS Research

9th Scandinavian Conference
on Information Systems, SCIS 2018
Odder, Denmark, August 5–8, 2018
Proceedings

 Springer

Editors
Sune Dueholm Müller (iD)
Aarhus University
Aarhus
Denmark

Jeppe Agger Nielsen (iD)
Department of Political Science
Aalborg University
Aalborg
Denmark

ISSN 1865-1348   ISSN 1865-1356   (electronic)
Lecture Notes in Business Information Processing
ISBN 978-3-319-96366-2   ISBN 978-3-319-96367-9   (eBook)
https://doi.org/10.1007/978-3-319-96367-9

Library of Congress Control Number: 2018948222

Printed on acid-free paper

This Springer imprint is published by the registered company Springer International Publishing AG
part of Springer Nature
The registered company address is: Gewerbestrasse 11, 6330 Cham, Switzerland

Preface

The 9th Scandinavian Conference on Information Systems (SCIS9), 2018, was held in Odder, Denmark, and was organized by the Department of Management at Aarhus University.

SCIS9 emphasized digital adaptation, disruption, and survival as overall themes. Digital innovation impacts all aspects of society, and organizations are forced to use and adapt digital technology in their fight for survival in the face of digital disruption. Digital innovation and transformation is no longer reserved for the most daring businesses. Those who fail to innovate and embrace digital technology may be left behind and go out of business. According to The World Economic Forum, we are at the beginning of the Fourth Industrial Revolution. As a consequence of digital disruption, "just over half of the names of companies on the Fortune 500 have disappeared since the year 2000."[1] Organizations are looking for ways to keep up with fast-paced changes in customer demands, apply new technology in novel ways, and transform their businesses. However, as organizations strive to transform themselves, they often face significant challenges, obstacles, and unintended consequences that require an understanding of the role of digital technologies. By selecting "Digital Adaptation, Disruption, and Survival" as the conference theme, we wanted to encourage researchers to address questions such as: What do the concepts of "digital innovation," "digital disruption," and "digital transformation" actually mean? Which industries and organizations—private or public—are affected and how? How does digital technology impact business models and support new forms of consumption, such as those made possible by the sharing economy? What are the downsides and critical aspects of current developments?

A total of 18 papers were submitted to the conference. The evaluation was a double-blind review process with two reviewers for each manuscript. Finally, five papers were accepted for presentation at the conference and published in these proceedings (acceptance rate of 28%).

SCIS9 proudly presented three keynote speakers: Richard L. Baskerville from Georgia State University (USA), Nils Fonstad from the MIT Center for Information System Research (USA), and Tina Blegind Jensen from Copenhagen Business School (Denmark). As in previous years, the SCIS conference was organized in conjunction with the Information Systems Research Conference in Scandinavia (IRIS) with its 41th annual meeting.

---

[1] https://www.weforum.org/agenda/2016/01/digital-disruption-has-only-just-begun/.

We are thankful to all those people who contributed to this conference as organizers, Program Committee members, and reviewers. We would also like to thank Springer for the very fruitful and easy collaboration. Finally, we would like to say thanks to all the volunteers who contributed to making this conference a memorable event.

May 2018   Jeppe Agger Nielsen
                                                                 Sune Dueholm Müller

Organization

Conference Chairs

Bjarne Rerup Schlichter   Aarhus University, Denmark
Lise Tordrup Heeager   Aarhus University, Denmark

Program Chairs

Sune Dueholm Müller   Aarhus University, Denmark
Jeppe Agger Nielsen   Aalborg University, Denmark

Proceedings Chairs

Sune Dueholm Müller   Aarhus University, Denmark
Jeppe Agger Nielsen   Aalborg University, Denmark

Web Chair

Merete Elmann   Aarhus University, Denmark

Keynotes and Symposium Chair

Andrea Carugati   Aarhus University, Denmark

Program Committee

Per Svejvig   Aarhus University, Denmark
Karin Hørup   Aarhus University, Denmark

.

Contents

Experiencing Expectations: Extending the Concept of UX Anticipation

Thomas Lindgren[1,2(✉)], Magnus Bergquist[1], Sarah Pink[3],
Martin Berg[4], and Vaike Fors[1]

[1] Halmstad University, Box 823, 301 18 Halmstad, Sweden
thomas.lindgren@volvocars.com,
{magnus.bergquist,vaike.fors}@hh.se
[2] Volvo Car Corporation, 405 31 Göteborg, Sweden
[3] School of Media and Communication, RMIT University,
GPO Box 2476, Melbourne, VIC 3001, Australia
sarah.pink@rmit.edu.au
[4] Department of Computer Science and Media Technology,
Malmö University, 205 06 Malmö, Sweden
martin.berg@mah.se

Abstract. This paper demonstrates the role of pre-product user experience (UX) in product design. For automotive companies, questions concerning how users will experience not yet available products is pressing - due to an increase in UX design for products, combined with a decrease in time-to-market for new products. Conventional UX research provides insights through investigating specific situated moments during use, or users' reflections after use, yet cannot provide knowledge about how users will engage with not yet existing products. To understand pre-product UX we undertook a netnographic study of three people's experiences of expecting and owning a Tesla car. We identified how modes of anticipation evolve before using the actual car, through online social interaction, creating a pre-product experience. The study offers a foundation for theorizing pre-product UX as socially generated anticipated UX, as well as insights for UX design in industry.

Keywords: User experience · Expectations · Automotive · Anticipation

1 Introduction

The pervasive spread of digitalization and automation changes the conditions in which cars can be experienced, used and become part of everyday life [1]. This paper responds to the growing demand for broadening existing definitions of user experience within the automotive industry by outlining how pre-product user experiences can inform User Experience (UX) design. It proposes a new mode of what Yogasara et al. [2] has called anticipated user experience (AUX). Whereas in previous accounts of UX expectations are assumed to take place before an actual experience (anticipated UX) [3–5], we argue that perceived expectations can be redefined as pre-product experiences. To develop this argument and discussion we report on a study of pre-product

S. D. Müller and J. A. Nielsen (Eds.): SCIS 2018, LNBIP 326, pp. 1–13, 2018.
https://doi.org/10.1007/978-3-319-96367-9_1

experience amongst expectant users of Tesla cars, which demonstrates how anticipation is an important element of user experience itself, rather than being prior to it.

UX design is an increasingly important factor for competitive product development in the automotive industry. Research shows that implementation of features and usability testing is not sufficient to attract future customers who are increasingly faced with different and competing offers [6, 7]. Although UX is often defined as holistic in the sense that it aims at understanding how people relate to and experience products in various contexts [6], research [8] and industry trends [1, 9] have indicated that the UX communities and consequentially the automotive industry need to refine their current understandings of how pre-product experiences are shaped and how they affect people's expectations of anticipated products. UX often engages with questions of emotion and affect as well as the situatedness and temporality of experiences [6, 8], yet often with an emphasis on how people relate to and experience a product in the present. Despite the widely spread acknowledgement that user experiences often change over time [6, 10], UX has largely focused on situated experiences during or after use of a particular product. However, this perspective limits the extent to which we can understand how emerging and not yet experienced products will be engaged with by customers [11, 12]. There is moreover a lack of HCI research into how the connected car is experienced and becomes integrated into people's everyday lives [13].

In a contemporary context of digital materiality, where the digital and material worlds and experiences can no longer be considered to be separate from each other [14], pre-product experiences are already emerging as people generate ways of sharing and coordinating their anticipatory modes of engagement with products online. Our research examined this through the research question: *How do users pre-product experiences shape product anticipation?* To develop our analysis we took a generative ethnographic approach [15] based on a netnographic study [16] of how pre-product user experience develops in an online Tesla owners forum. This enabled us to follow in detail how three Tesla owners' expectations and experiences developed through their forum interactions. We demonstrate how this focus on Anticipated User Experience (AUX) extends current research on user experience to involve users' digital experiences and expectations of products at a very early stage. Our research suggests that consumer product companies, like the automotive industry should begin to treat anticipation as part of the UX design process and design for user's pre-product expectations as well as for the experience of use.

The paper is organized as follows. First, we review relevant work on UX frameworks and anticipated UX. We contextualize the social nature of anticipation through a sociological approach to AUX, followed by the research design and results. We conclude by discussing the implications of anticipation for future research and UX design.

2   Literature Review

2.1   Changing Conditions for Experiencing the Car

Digitalization and automation of the car, and the emerging vision of car as a service-provider as much as a means of transportation, has changed how people use, experience and expect the car to become part of their everyday lives. Three core aspects of these changes that impact on how the car is perceived, used and experienced are identified in existing literature. These changes demand new ways of understanding how pre-product user experience is created and developed in order to attract customers and provide positive user experience [8, 17].

First, there is a shift from the physical product as involving a standalone product experience towards a more service-dominated experience which is integrated with the user's everyday life [18]. Subscription based models, in combination with digital services, generate innovative solutions for new forms of car-on-demand accessed as flexible services through apps. From the user perspective this means more options become available and there is a shorter time for anticipation and expectations to develop before making a selection [19].

Second, automotive trends in online product stores, instead of traditional dealerships, and in-app add-on functionality integrated with other services extend the physical experience of the car into a digital platform. This changes the user's first expectations and experiences of what would conventionally have been a material technology purchased in a face-to-face context into a digital experience. How this affects the overall experience and development of expectations has not been fully explored [20]. The effect of digitalization is also increased through use of social media and a shift in how a user's future car can be experienced. This creates new social interactions between users of the same type of products or services, which enhances and extends the pre-product experience before its actual use.

Third, software updates during the car's life-time [21] based on AI technologies enable the car to adapt to individual needs and behaviours. This provides UX designers with new possibilities to continually enhance users' expectations and experiences [21, 22].

2.2   Anticipation and User Experience

UX is defined by the ISO standard as "[a] person's perceptions and responses that result from the use and/or anticipated use of a product, system or service" [23]. This definition is widely shared within the industry and in UX research [3]. The phase before actual use, and how this phase relates to later experiences, has often been difficult to define and has not been acknowledged as part of the actual experience. Subsequently, this phase has not been investigated little [24]. However, the ISO definition introduces the concept of anticipated use, and it is visualized in some UX frameworks [4], as in Fig. 1 below.

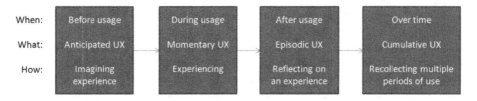

Fig. 1. Phases of UX, adapted after Roto et al. [5]

Research that engages with anticipated use [2, 24] understands anticipated UX (AUX) as people's anticipation of the future product or service and how it is influenced by people's imaginations, desires, expectations and already existing experiences. Yogasara et al. [2] defines four factors that influence AUX: the users intended use, the user profile, the user's experiential knowledge and the user's anticipated emotions. Recent research on AUX [24] takes a cause and effect perspective in isolation from the dynamics of the social context. UX research also tends to make a distinction between experiencing momentary UX (the physical product) or AUX (the imaginary product). However, when product experiences extend and appear both in physical and digital forms, the idea of boundaries between the physical and imaginary become unclear and lead to implications both for UX design and for how designers conceptualize AUX. Not only do digitalization and the possibilities of sharing the experiences through social media shift the focus and importance of UX to the phase of AUX, social aspects will also play a more important role [25]. We therefore suggest that anticipated user experiences should not be studied as an individual user-product relationship, but as a shared social activity involving multiple and changing relationships. In the next section we propose a theoretical framework to approach shared anticipation and UX.

2.3   Theorizing Anticipation

In this paper, we draw on a sociological theory of anticipation to understand the early phases of users' expectations and experiences of a product and how it relates to cultural and social aspects of what users do and experience when coordinating their futures. Tavory and Eliasoph [26] have defined the concept of human anticipation through three categories or modes:

- Protentions – Which defines our actions or next move. This is the anticipation we take for granted and use when we experience the present. E.g. when we aim to hit a tennis ball with the racket.
- Trajectories – Where people in search of meaning make narratives or projects that have a beginning, middle and end. Our actions become a part of the process to advance the trajectory.
- Plans and temporal landscapes – How we coordinate according to less intentional plans or things treated as inevitably already defined and natural e.g. calendar time, cosmic, eternal, religious related events.

Tavory and Eliasoph argue that rather than these different modes being mutually interdependent and co-constituting, they can instead coexist and are sometimes shared between people. To anticipate the future, several trajectories and plans become active, and people manage to quickly switch between these different modes. This theory expands the view of anticipation in three ways. First, it shows that some actions are based on our "feeling" in the moment, which might not be fully reflected on and is constantly calibrated in our interactions according to the specific situation. Thus, we might not always act predictably or according to a model. Second, by revealing the importance of our plans, with a beginning and an end, we make sense of each of our actions (protentions). Without a trajectory or a plan our actions will not make sense to us, which means that our interactions with a product are part of a plan. Third, the complex and simultaneous ways these trajectories and plans are managed makes it obvious how difficult it is to model UX in cause and effect frameworks. There are many things going on in a user's mind, and the interaction with a product is just one of several trajectories and plans happening simultaneously.

This understanding of anticipation enables us to understand the user's relationship to a product or service through a focus on how the user's interactions with the product become meaningful as elements in the user's own plan or trajectory. While the temporalities of UX have been identified [10, 12], most existing research investigates the phases where users are actually interacting with physical products or later reflecting on these interactions. This existing work tends to focus on user's emotions and product attributes in the use of the product [27] or on how the user's motivation participates in UX [28], rather than describing the evolution of experiences and expectations.

To summarize the advances made in UX research towards understanding pre-product experiences and expectations, existing research has sought to define the characteristics of the concept of AUX but has not situated anticipation and expectations as elements in the total user experience, whether the product is experienced in physical or digital forms. This raises two points that inform our work:

First, a social science perspective offers us a way to advance UX research towards a renewed AUX approach, which analyses how user anticipation affects the choice of a product or service. Here, we show how this can be mobilized through the example of how users experience the anticipation of a complex product - a Tesla car.

Second, if we take anticipation seriously then we need to consider not only how products are imagined before use, but also the experience of engaging with a product before it is used. This goes beyond seeing anticipation as prior to the user's experience of a product to instead see it as part of the user experience. This led us to investigate how an anticipatory online product experience might be analysed as an experience in itself for individual users and co-users, through an analysis of how aspiration and anticipation of a new product/service constituted user experience.

3 Research Design

To identify pre-product experience, we took an exploratory inductive approach through a netnographic study [16] in a Swedish Tesla owners forum during 10 months in 2017–18. We selected Tesla, because the brand provides one of the most progressive cars with advanced automotive technologies and moreover has a model for marketing and sales that differs from the traditional automotive industry [29]. The forum [http://teslaclubsweden.se] was selected so we could follow how Tesla owner's expectations and experiences evolved through the ownership process, through interactions with other forum participants. Similar to other netnographic studies of interactions in online communities (for instance [30, 31]), this study engaged both with participants' ongoing activity in the community and their previous conversations. The method allowed us to discover how user expectations and user experience gradually unfolded over time through the conversations without having to interfere in social interactions and anticipatory conversations.

Data collection and analysis was undertaken in two steps. First we were immersed in the community to gain a basic overview of the forum (around 4000 members at the time of study), the forum structure, member activities and the general atmosphere. We analysed 28 recently updated member presentations and 25 popular discussions. Identified themes were e.g. reasons for becoming Tesla owners, how Tesla owners like to drive, debates on fully autonomous driving, and access to beta software. The most significant quotations were transcribed for the second step in the analysis, which focused on how Tesla ownership developed over time. Based on the themes identified in step one, three active and long-term (over 2 years) forum members were selected. A selection criteria was that the user had actually bought a Tesla while being active in the community. We analysed how their anticipation evolved over time, from when they entered the forum until becoming Tesla owners. Their personal presentation threads and additional threads were collected and their expectations and experiences through the ownership phases and transitions were analysed. Informed consent was gathered from the participants through private messages in the forum. We used Atlas.ti for coding based on thematic analysis [32] to group emerging themes, including imagining the future, ordering process, sharing expectations, picking up the car and the new Tesla life.

4   Results

The Tesla forum is an open and active online forum that attracts one third of Swedish Tesla car owners as members, as well as people with a general interest in the company, the car itself, and people interested in new energy solutions and electric vehicles (EV's). The atmosphere in the forum is very social and inviting to new curious members and the community quickly replies and encourages them to become Tesla owners.

Our findings indicate that the experience of becoming a Tesla owner is a three-phase process: (a) imagining the future, (b) sharing experiences and expectations, (c) living the new life. These different modes of anticipation become experiences that can develop over time.

Based on the initial analysis we chose three active Tesla forum participants to deepen the analysis of how individual Tesla expectations and experiences develops over time. The results show that this was a highly interactive process based on sharing information and attuning with other members. The following sections describe each phase more in detail.

4.1   Imagining the Future

The first phase of the emergent identity as a Tesla owner often starts with becoming part of a cult of the future, organized around writings about the inventor and leader of Tesla, Elon Musk. Their stories range through being part of a social movement, seeing the Tesla as the ultimate driving experience, and the Tesla car being the materialization of this anticipated future. A current Tesla owner describes how his expectations from the beginning were not of the car itself: *"Tesla is not a car but a "concept" that I wanted to experience before I get too old"*. The imagination of the future visions leads to a search for more information to learn about how a Tesla car could fit into this imagined future.

The Tesla owner Carl's story exemplifies how anticipating participation in a transformation towards a future vision shapes into a more concrete vision of owning a Tesla car. His interest in computers and space led him to imagine himself as a Tesla owner. As such, he would be part of Elon Musk's visions and plans for the SpaceX project and his vision about colonizing Mars. He joined the Tesla forum almost secretly: *"Got deep down into Tesla and began in secret to read this excellent forum (which, incidentally, has a really good atmosphere)"*. Eventually the idea of buying a Tesla came as a materialization of his imagination of a future culture which aimed to transform the world with technology for the benefit of the environment.

The Tesla owner Dennis described his experiences of his first test drive of a Tesla Model S in the forum. Since that day, he decided to get one, no matter what it would take. His anticipation was fuelled with real experience of the car and a conviction that the new technologies of EV-cars is the ultimate solution for future mobility, and that Tesla is the materialization of this vision. *"Getting new gadgets is the best. A Tesla is frankly speaking the ultimate gadget."* Tesla owner John exemplifies anticipation of the car as a radical reconceptualization of what a car is about: *"I have always had a HUGE interest in cars ... However, it has been more like "the bigger engine and the more noise they make the better" ... and it will be difficult to change mindset, I think!"* Since his first test drive of a Tesla, he was convinced that the car was amazing, but planned to keep his "V8 muscle car" while figuring out how the Tesla Model S would fit into his lifestyle.

All these stories of anticipation are concrete experiences of real and imagined cars, and thus building blocks in socially constructed stories, supported by digital tools on the Tesla website to envision and design what participants saw as the ultimate car. Together with the social interactions in the online community they enhance the possibilities for anticipation of the future, even if the actual car is not experienced in real life.

4.2   Sharing Experiences and Expectations

Visioning is about defining goals and shaping a repertoire of needs and wants. But, to become tools for action, needs must be organized into series of actions that form trajectories, which lead the forum user towards realizing the anticipated goal when pressing the button to order a new car. Creating and sharing logics of argumentation was important for how users co-constructed and shaped the trajectories that emerged in the forum.

An illustrating example is Carl's emergent narrative of how he could fit a Tesla into his everyday life, which was jointly developed with other forum members. The trajectory formed around arguments that were initially disparate, but in discussions became aligned and mutually supporting. They discussed the value of money, what an electric car could save in terms of cost for fuel, the future of charging stations, and technology development in general. Eventually, this created both a logical sequence of arguments supporting the choice of a Tesla, and the timing for action to maximize the experience: *"The Swedish krona is falling against the dollar, approaching a price increase tomorrow, and the end of free SuC (Super Charging stations) made me buy now. I ordered a 60D in Midnight Silver Metallic and Autopilot, now I just hope the "old" textile seats run out so I get the premium seats as bonus."* Sharing his ideas in the forum had two consequences. First, it clarified and enabled him to reflect on his vague thoughts and ideas; second it made ideas available for other users and served to influence and adapt their expectations. Eventually it seemed inevitable both for him and his peers that he would purchase a car that entirely overshadowed his originally anticipated rational car choice.

Sharing not only introduces new activities that emerge and create new experiences, it also organizes the experiences onto a path. Forum members compare delivery dates, share ownership tips and invite each other to meet and offer charging possibilities in their homes. Dennis made detailed financing worksheets that he gladly shared with others at the same stage. Although he found the waiting process *"unbearably"* long it created an exciting and pleasurable experience since he could access digital content online and share experiences with others: *"Thankfully, the Model S is a car with a lot of enthusiasts, so it is certainly not short on information and videos to dig into online"*. To know every step in the production and delivery process, Dennis created *"a script that checks the status every 30 min and sends a mess to my phone if it is changed, so I know it for sure"*. This script was shared and appreciated by other members. Sharing the waiting process creates joyful competition between members waiting for the same model, as Dennis put it: *"It looks like you are winning who owns a Tesla first"*. Sharing time to delivery together with digital representations of the built car builds up the expectations of the actual materialization of the artefact. Dennis was instantly obliged to share photos on receiving his car, *"Pics or it didn't happen."* The pre-product experience culminates in this performative ritual of taking and sharing photos of the car's delivery, through which it is celebrated by the online community.

4.3 Living the New Life

Actual owners of Tesla cars are respected and very important to the forum members' ability to anticipate and experience, as they provide the community with hands on experiences. Real use of the car after the pick-up is often referred to as the life changing "new Tesla life". Dennis was very satisfied with the car and how it met his expectations of the ultimate gadget. *"I already love the car. Madly in love. It is incredibly good. I can't understand how they could get that much coolness in one package. A couple of small details, however, stuck out. I felt some vibration at low speeds, most around 30–50, so that the head like bobbing against the headrest... Should it be like that?"* By sharing the part of the experience that did not meet his expectations, he instantly got feedback from other Tesla owners who shared their experience and tips to solve or reduce his worries and recalibrate his anticipations. A year after the delivery, John showed his love for his new Tesla and posted a long story of the first year's experiences, where he intended *"to make a small tribute thread with pictures of her and our relationship here!"* It is narrated as a family photo album, very personal with a sense of humour in the description of his relation to the car, and provides other members with a digest of experiences over time.

Simultaneously, the Tesla is positively described as an expanding technology that is updated and provided with new functionality long after the customer receives the car. John posts after a software update: *"It's exciting with new updates during the car's life. Both functionality and visually"*. Through continuous software updates experiences of anticipation evolve over time. In the forum there is continuous discussion about future releases and indulgence of software glitches in current versions that nevertheless results in trust in the company as a premium brand even though some functionality is delayed. As such, the three owners discussed here developed a relationship to the car, the other community members and to the brand itself as a "total Tesla ownership experience."

5   Discussion

This paper has outlined how pre-product user experiences can inform UX design and has proposed a new mode of AUX. In a context of digital materiality the conditions for experiencing cars are changing, and there is a need to refine current understandings of UX for the automotive industry and UX communities. We propose treating anticipation as part of the UX design process in order to design for user's pre-product expectations. The Tesla owners' narratives demonstrated that the anticipated UX of their ordered car and the initiation of the relation with it, social interaction in the community, and digital aspects of the car, all participate in shaping anticipation. Tavory and Eliasoph's [26] framework of anticipation, enabled us to generate new insights concerning the social and temporal aspects and complexity of AUX.

5.1   Importance of Trajectories and Plans

The starting point for these owners' journeys to becoming Tesla owners begins in their anticipation of overarching trajectories or plans of the future ranging from getting into the Elon Musk culture, a full EV future or the multipurpose tool for driving experiences. The AUX expressed here is described in different imaginative descriptions and getting the car is a key protention forward on their trajectory or plan. For each individual this could involve several ongoing or emerging uncoupled trajectories, like being able to finance the cost of ownership, solve everyday transportation needs, having a unique driving experience or fitting the users image and beliefs. By making protentions in posting and sharing their anticipation with others the multiple ongoing trajectories change and converge into an almost inevitable plan where the action of pushing the order button makes total sense even if the rational arguments sometimes say something different.

5.2   Feel in the Moment

The digitalization of the car and use of the community as platform enhance sharing the experience and create many new experiences and trajectories based on users' own creativity around the anticipated car, e.g. financing formulas, software scripts for instant delivery updates or delivery competitions. These protentions are not always possible to predict or refer to a well prepared trajectory or plan that could be explained in a model, but rather emerge based on the persons "feel" in the moment. The digital platform encourages sharing spontaneous protentions in the emerging discussions. The possibilities with digitalization and subscription based ownership models of the car that encourage feel in the moment protentions, will be more important to understand in relation to UX.

5.3 Managing Trajectories and Plans Simultaneously

There are many simultaneously ongoing trajectories and plans for the owners, which highlight the difficulties in viewing the UX of the car solely through a cause and effect model for user-car relations in a specific context. The fast sharing of the members' experiences and expectations through the community evolve, converge or emerge the trajectories and plans for each individual in unpredictable ways, which creates and adds new experiences and expectations to the overall user experience. Continuous evolution of the products' functionality during use, through software updates, also encourages anticipation of new trajectories to be created and provides possibilities for positive experiences.

5.4 Advancing UX Research

To sum up, the concept of AUX [2], has not fully accounted for anticipation and expectation in relation to the user's management of multiple ongoing trajectories, plans or instant protentions shared in the social interactions within the forum or for whether the product is experienced in physical or digital forms. A social and temporal perspective provides a new approach that advances UX research beyond the current more static user-product perspective. Figure 2 shows a user trajectory towards Tesla ownership developed in the forum. During the process the digital Tesla transformed into a materialized reality, which fed experiences of anticipation to new members and enabled their imaginations of future Tesla ownership.

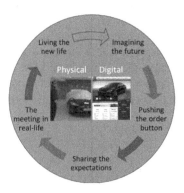

Fig. 2. The trajectory of evolving ownership anticipation.

As Fig. 2 shows, the first phase of anticipation in the process of buying a Tesla car grew from the owner's urge to be a part of, or to experience, something more than just the car itself. Here the experience within the community became shared anticipation and expectation of an imagined car. This created multiple member activities and generated tangible positive experiences for the users. Based on the empirical study, we argue that there is a need to expand the view of UX concepts. Cause and effect models, such as CUE or similar models used in recent UX research claim to be holistic [11], but do not really explain the social effects of anticipation in pre-product experience. More research on AUX is needed to strengthen the understanding of a holistic view of UX. To achieve this requires expanding the understanding of how users' social activities in pre-product experiences shape UX. When we re-conceptualise the experience of a product, from being only physical towards including both digital and social experience, the boundaries between the physical and the non-physical UX change for both the user and the product industry. We used netnography as an approach through which to learn about lead-users' social activities and product anticipations, but further investigation is needed to advance our understandings of how to better involve users in the development of UX. Better awareness of pre-product user anticipation is likely to increase possibilities to design holistic UX solutions to meet the automotive transformation from product to services, increased digitalisation, and intelligent evolving functionality.

6   Conclusions

This paper has examined how users pre-product experiences shape product anticipation. We used Tavory and Eliasoph's theory of social anticipation [26] to identify user trajectories towards their decision to order a Tesla car. The results show that digitalization of the user experience enable experiences to emerge in the process of anticipation in two ways: first, the online forum affords sharing, commenting and interaction through which anticipation is co-operatively shaped in multiple situations; second, the high digitalization of the Tesla car blurs the line between physical and virtual experiences. These experiences can have shorter (protention) or longer (plans) perspectives. Users multiple and evolving trajectories of anticipation can align over time and strengthen the experience of the product, and thus enhance expectations. Aligned anticipation can bring users closer to implementing the anticipated future. Finally, the study adds to the theorizing of anticipation of UX in HCI research. While existing approaches to AUX are based on theories of cause and effect relationships, this study shows the value of social theories for understanding the dynamics of user's contexts and ongoing social activities of sharing physical and virtual experiences, involving multiple and changing relationships. The results have implications for product development. The study identified no clear boundaries between people's imaginaries, expectations and desires of future products, and the ongoing socially shaped and emergent experiences of the product, in its physical or digital form. Instead, such experiences seem important for how goals are formed and decisions are made, and are ongoing in the pre-product phase, thus making anticipation important for product UX design.

References

1. Gao, P., Kaas, H.-W., Mohr, D., Wee, D.: Automotive revolution: perspective towards 2030: how the convergence of disruptive technology-driven trends could transform the auto industry. Advanced Industries. McKinsey and Company, Advanced Industries (2016)
2. Yogasara, T., Popovic, V., Kraal, B.J., Chamorro-Koc, M.: General characteristics of anticipated user experience (AUX) with interactive products. In: Proceedings of IASDR2011: The 4th World Conference on Design Research: Diversity and Unity, IASDR, pp. 1–11 (2011)
3. Law, E.L.-C., Roto, V., Hassenzahl, M., Vermeeren, A.P.O.S., Kort, J.: Understanding, scoping and defining user experience: a survey approach. In: Proceedings of the SIGCHI Conference on Human Factors in Computing Systems, Boston, MA, USA, pp. 719–728. ACM (2009)
4. Pohlmeyer, A.E., Hecht, M., Blessing, L.: User experience lifecycle model ContinUE [Continuous user experience]. In: Der Mensch im Mittepunkt technischer Systeme. Fortschritt-Berichte VDI Reihe, vol. 22, pp. 314–317 (2009)
5. Roto, V., Law, E., Vermeeren, A., Hoonhout, J.: User experience white paper–bringing clarity to the concept of user experience (2011)
6. Hassenzahl, M., Tractinsky, N.: User experience - a research agenda. Behav. Inf. Technol. **25**, 91–97 (2006)
7. Väänänen-Vainio-Mattila, K., Roto, V., Hassenzahl, M.: Now let's do it in practice: user experience evaluation methods in product development. In: CHI 2008 Extended Abstracts on Human Factors in Computing Systems, Florence, Italy, pp. 3961–3964. ACM (2008)
8. Allam, A., Dahlan, H.M.: User experience: challenges and opportunities. J. Inf. Syst. Res. Innov. **3**, 28–36 (2013)
9. State of UX in 2018. https://uxdesign.cc/on-why-we-write-the-words-we-write-the-way-we-write-them-8423f4734e77
10. Karapanos, E., Zimmerman, J., Forlizzi, J., Martens, J.-B.: User experience over time: an initial framework. In: Proceedings of the SIGCHI Conference on Human Factors in Computing Systems, Boston, MA, USA, pp. 729–738. ACM (2009)
11. Minge, M., Thüring, M.: Hedonic and pragmatic halo effects at early stages of user experience. Int. J. Hum. Comput. Stud. **109**, 13–25 (2018)
12. Pettersson, I.: The temporality of in-vehicle user experience. Division Design & Human Factors Department of Product and Production Development. Chalmers University of Technology (2016)
13. Svangren, M.K., Skov, M.B., Kjeldskov, J.: The connected car: an empirical study of electric cars as mobile digital devices. In: Proceedings of the 19th International Conference on Human-Computer Interaction with Mobile Devices and Services, Vienna, Austria, pp. 1–12. ACM (2017)
14. Pink, S., Ardèvol, E., Lanzeni, D.: Digital materiality. In: Pink, S., Ardevol, E., Lanzeni, D. (eds.) Digital Materialities: Design and Anthropology, Bloomsbury, London, pp. 1–26 (2016)
15. Dourish, P.: Responsibilities and implications: further thoughts on ethnography and design. In: Proceedings of the 2007 Conference on Designing for User eXperiences, Chicago, Illinois, pp. 2–16. ACM (2007)
16. Kozinets, R.V.: Netnography. In: The International Encyclopedia of Digital Communication and Society. Wiley (2015)
17. Bødker, S.: When second wave HCI meets third wave challenges. In: Proceedings of the 4th Nordic Conference on Human-Computer Interaction: Changing Roles, pp. 1–8. ACM (2006)

18. Lusch, R.F., Vargo, S.L.: Service-dominant logic: reactions, reflections and refinements. Mark. Theory **6**, 281–288 (2006)
19. Garbarino, E., Johnson, M.S.: The different roles of satisfaction, trust, and commitment in customer relationships. J. Mark. **63**, 70–87 (1999)
20. Immonen, M., Sintonen, S., Koivuniemi, J.: The value of human interaction in service channels. Comput. Hum. Behav. **78**, 316–325 (2018)
21. Lyyra, A.K., Koskinen, K.M.: The ambivalent characteristics of connected, digitised products: case Tesla Model S. In: Lundh Snis, U. (ed.) SCIS 2016. LNBIP, vol. 259, pp. 57–69. Springer, Cham (2016). https://doi.org/10.1007/978-3-319-43597-8_5
22. Gomes, C.C., Preto, S.: Artificial intelligence and interaction design for a positive emotional user experience. In: Karwowski, W., Ahram, T. (eds.) IHSI 2018. AISC, vol. 722, pp. 62–68. Springer, Cham (2018). https://doi.org/10.1007/978-3-319-73888-8_11
23. Ergonomics of human system interaction - Part 210: human-centred design for interactive systems. International Organization for Standardization (ISO), vol. ISO 9241-210 (2010)
24. Eilu, E.: Using cognitive psychology to understand anticipated user experience in computing products. In: Mobile Platforms, Design, and Apps for Social Commerce, pp. 175–196. IGI Global (2017)
25. Goh, K.-Y., Heng, C.-S., Lin, Z.: Social media brand community and consumer behavior: quantifying the relative impact of user- and marketer-generated content. Inf. Syst. Res. **24**, 88–107 (2013)
26. Tavory, I., Eliasoph, N.: Coordinating futures: toward a theory of anticipation. Am. J. Sociol. **118**(4), 908–942 (2013)
27. Hassenzahl, M.: The thing and I: understanding the relationship between user and product. In: Blythe, M.A., Overbeeke, K., Monk, A.F., Wright, P.C. (eds.) Funology: From Usability to Enjoyment. HCIS, vol. 3, pp. 31–42. Springer, Dordrecht (2005). https://doi.org/10.1007/1-4020-2967-5_4
28. Hassenzahl, M., Schöbel, M., Trautmann, T.: How motivational orientation influences the evaluation and choice of hedonic and pragmatic interactive products: the role of regulatory focus. Interact. Comput. **20**, 473–479 (2008)
29. Zucchi, K.: What Makes Tesla's Business Model Different? Investopedia (2018)
30. Hewer, P., Brownlie, D.: Cultures of consumption of car aficionados: aesthetics and consumption communities. Int. J. Sociol. Soc. Policy **27**, 106–119 (2007)
31. Schembri, S., Latimer, L.: Online brand communities: constructing and co-constructing brand culture. J. Mark. Manag. **32**, 628–651 (2016)
32. Braun, V., Clarke, V.: Using thematic analysis in psychology. Qual. Res. Psychol. **3**, 77–101 (2006)

Recognizing and Mitigating the Negative Effects of Information Technology Use: A Systematic Review of Persuasive Characteristics in Information Systems

Liisa Kuonanoja[✉] and Harri Oinas-Kukkonen

Faculty of Information Technology and Electrical Engineering, OASIS,
University of Oulu, Pentti Kaiteran katu 1, 90570 Oulu, Finland
{liisa.kuonanoja, harri.oinas-kukkonen}@oulu.fi

Abstract. Although information systems and technology have brought many benefits into people's everyday lives, not to mention society as a whole, they are also accompanied by negative consequences. For example, technostress, anxiety, and even different kinds of addictions are among the side effects of information technology use. Clearly, such negative consequences cannot be fully avoided, but at least some of them may be mitigated via good system design. In this study, we addressed the dark side of information technology use in everyday life and in a leisure context, reviewing contributions from the basket of eight information systems journals published between 2004 and early 2018. In our analysis, we utilized the Persuasive Systems Design model in order to recognize and analyze information system characteristics that may mitigate the negative consequences of information technology use.

Keywords: Dark side · Negative consequences · Persuasive technology
Persuasive system design model

1 Introduction

In recent decades, the way we live and work has been revolutionized. Information systems (IS) have brought transformational benefits to individuals, organizations, and even society as a whole [1, p. 58]. However, these benefits have not come without a cost, which is the dark side of IS. With the increased use of information technology (IT), undesirable side effects are also increasing. Recognizing such negative consequences and making improvements to system design could help researchers to identify new ways to reduce the potential harm caused by IS. As yet, there is a lack of literature on this topic; however, some of the harmful and even damaging consequences of IS use have already been identified [2, 3]. It is hoped that these consequences can be mitigated, if not prevented.

The negative effects of IS may be apparent at both individual and organizational levels, leading to negative societal effects on a large scale. For example, decreased job satisfaction as well as organizational and continuance commitment [4], anxiety [5], and problems with everyday life and social relations [6] are among the negative consequences

© Springer International Publishing AG, part of Springer Nature 2018
S. D. Müller and J. A. Nielsen (Eds.): SCIS 2018, LNBIP 326, pp. 14–25, 2018.
https://doi.org/10.1007/978-3-319-96367-9_2

of IT use. This paper focuses solely on negative effects at the individual level. Another group of negative consequences of IT usage may arise from users behaving maliciously toward others via IT [1, p. 178]. Examples of this include cyberbullying and the hacking of systems belonging to individuals or organizations. Such malicious actions, in which an individual comes to harm as a result of another person's conduct rather than from their use of IT *per se*, are beyond the scope of this paper.

In this study, we have focused on voluntary IT use for non-organizational purposes. The specific aim of this paper was to identify software features and qualities that may mitigate the negative consequences of IS that have been identified in the literature. We achieved this by analyzing published articles from major scientific journals in the IS field.[1] The Persuasive Systems Design (PSD) model [7] has described a means for influencing IS users in a positive manner. We have argued that this model is a useful tool for determining which software features and qualities identified in earlier studies can be used in our research context. Thus, in this analysis, we utilized the PSD model as a lens through which to look at ways of mitigating the dark side of IT use.

2   Background

2.1   The Dark Side of Information Systems

The use of IT carries consequences for individuals and, eventually, for the whole of society. Although the benefits of technology are often emphasized, there are also many negative effects. The dark side of IT use has been defined by Tarafdar et al. [2] as "a broad collection of 'negative' phenomena that are associated with the use of IT, and that have the potential to infringe the well-being of individuals, organizations and societies." The first studies on these negative effects were conducted over 30 years ago, and they mostly focused on workplace and organizational contexts [2]. The scope of research has since broadened to include leisure IT use [3].

Naturally, new negative consequences will continue to arise as IT evolves. In a study by Pirkkalainen and Salo [3], the majority of negative consequences of IT use fell under four categories: technostress, IT addiction, IT anxiety, and information overload. Technostress is stress experienced by an end user of IT [4]. End users may experience technostress in organizational contexts as a result of using work-related information and communication technology (see, for example, [4]) or in leisure contexts as a result of using, for instance, social networking sites (see, for example, [8]). Information overload occurs when IT provides too much information in comparison to a user's needs, thus overwhelming the user [3, 9].

Addiction may be associated with different types of IS, such as games (for example, [10]), social networking sites (for example, [11, 12]), online auction sites, or, more broadly, mobile phones and the internet. According to one definition of IT addiction, it is "a psychological dependency on IT that involves excessive and compulsive use despite significant negative consequences" [14]. In contrast, IT anxiety concerns an individual's willingness and ability to use IT [15]. People suffering from IT anxiety may avoid using

---

[1] http://aisnet.org/?SeniorScholarBasket

IT and may have difficulties understanding new technology. They may also feel apprehension when using IT [3]. There are also other kinds of negative consequences, such as loss of privacy and injuries related to poor ergonomics [2].

These consequences may impact individuals in many ways. Users may experience stress and their productivity may decrease [16], or they may become addicted to or obsessed with some element of IT, which could lead to obesity, decreased happiness, social isolation, and in the worst cases, even death [11]. It is evident that there is a need to find methods that mitigate the negative consequences of IT use.

2.2 Persuasive Systems Design

People often have a need to change aspects of their behavior or their attitudes, such as exercising more or using less plastic. Software design strategies used by persuasive technology can help people to change their attitudes or behavior [7]. According to the definition of persuasive technology, coercion and deception should not be used [7], rather the use of such systems should be voluntary in nature [17, 18]. Persuasive systems are often used in health-related systems, such as those that aid smoking cessation, or help individuals change their lifestyle in order to incorporate healthier habits [18, 19]. Persuasive systems have also been utilized in other domains, such as e-commerce and energy conservation.

The PSD model by Oinas-Kukkonen and Harjumaa is a tool for designing and evaluating persuasive systems [7]. The model consists of three phases that guide the designer through the system design process:

– The first phase, known as persuasion postulates, explains the main issues behind persuasive systems that relate to behavior change and IT, which the designer should understand before creating a new system. First, there is an understanding that IT is never neutral but that it always affects users in one way or another. Second, a user's commitment and cognitive consistency are needed for the change. Third, persuasion may happen through direct or indirect routes, and the route that is more effective depends on users' personal characteristics and the persuasion situation. Fourth, incremental steps toward the target behavior should be supported, since change is usually easier to achieve by taking small steps. Fifth, persuasion should be open and transparent, and designer bias should be revealed. Sixth, it is important for the system to be unobtrusive, because disturbing a user at an inopportune moment may result in unwanted outcomes. Finally, seventh, the system should be useful and easy to use [7].
– The second phase of the PSD model [7] focuses on examining the persuasion context to gain a comprehensive understanding of the situation in which the persuasion event will take place. The intent of the persuader and the type of change the system is supporting (whether this is a user's behavior or attitude) should be analyzed. The use, user, and technology context should be given attention to form a rigorous picture of the persuasion event. In addition, the strategy incorporating the main message and the route of persuasion should be designed. A system designed with such understanding will be more persuasive and fitting for the targeted users [7].
– The third phase consists of determining which software features will support users in approaching their behavior change objective. In the PSD model, such features are

divided into four categories, namely, primary task support, dialogue support, credibility support, and social influence. A new system does not need to incorporate all of these categories nor all of the features they contain, but their use will make it more persuasive [7]. The effects of software features have been investigated in numerous studies, such as [19, 20].

The factors mentioned in the PSD model are presented on a relatively abstract level, which leaves room for designers to interpret them. This means that the postulates can be taken into account and the chosen software system features can be implemented in a manner preferred by the design team.

3 Methods

As the basis for our research, we utilized a study previously carried out by Pirkkalainen and Salo [3], which was a literature review of the current state of dark side phenomena in IS that provided future directions for research. They concentrated their search on the basket of eight journals in IS research, because their objective was to focus on the main contributions to the IS field, which were likely to be in the field's leading journals [3].[2] The focus of their review was the negative effects of IT use on individuals in both leisure and organizational contexts. Searched material included all issues of the abovementioned journals from 1995 to 2015. Pirkkalainen and Salo [3] went through all journal issues without using a keyword search. Articles meeting the set criteria (studies addressing negative effect(s) of IT use on an individual) were included in their review.

In order to build on Pirkkalainen and Salo's [3] literature search, we used the same criteria in our study. We conducted a descriptive review [21] with a narrow scope in order to study our research objectives. We searched for articles issued between 2016 and early 2018, as these were published after the original research had been carried out. Contrary to Pirkkalainen and Salo [3], we concentrated only on articles investigating dark side effects in leisure contexts and excluded those in organizational contexts. As Pirkkalainen and Salo [3], we followed the main guidelines for literature review by Webster and Watson [22].

In the first round of our search, which was based on article titles, we found 39 new articles. We did not want to miss any relevant articles, so at this stage, we included articles about negative effects in organizational contexts. If an article was about the negative effects of IT use on individuals, then it was included, regardless of the context. After reviewing the abstracts and, if needed, the introductions, we included nine articles. To these, we added the 11 articles found by Pirkkalainen and Salo [3] relating to leisure/everyday contexts, bringing our data set to a total of 20 dark side articles.

---

[2] We utilized the basket of eight IS journals, which included the following top journals in the IS field: *MIS Quarterly, Information Systems Research, Journal of Management Information Systems, Journal of the Association for Information Systems, European Journal of Information Systems, Information Systems Journal, Journal of Information Technology,* and *Journal of Strategic Information Systems.* See: https://aisnet.org/?SeniorScholarBasket

We extracted effective software system features and qualities from analyzed articles and categorized them according to the PSD model. We exploited all three phases of the PSD model, which we used as main categories. The first category was persuasion postulates, the second was the persuasion context (the intent, event, and strategy), and the third was persuasive system features (primary task support, computer–human dialogue, perceived credibility, and social support).

Our objective was to identify software features and qualities that mitigated the negative consequences of IS use. We included features that provoked negative consequences in order to raise awareness of their need for mitigation. Of the 20 articles in our data set, 14 contained features that had some effect on the consequences of IS use. At this stage, we excluded six articles, as they did not discuss the three abovementioned phases but investigated, for example, users' feelings and qualifications (for example, [23]), or measured users' technostress reactions [24]. These six articles were not within the scope of our review.

4 Results

Our analysis of the dark side of IT use revealed meaningful findings. A summary of these findings has been presented in Table 1. Some of the postulates indicating the main issues behind persuasion systems had important mitigating effects on the negative consequences of IT use. The next biggest category with an effect was social support. In this category, features had negative consequences on IT users, although in one paper, social features were found to have a mitigating effect.

Of the 14 studies included in this review, nine described mitigation related to postulates in the PSD model [7]. The postulate stating that systems should be both useful and easy to use (including lack of errors and high quality information), was the most common mitigating quality. For example, Saunders et al. [25] mentioned that older users of mobile phones felt more easily overwhelmed by phones with a multitude of features compared to younger users. This finding is in line with suggestions made by the PSD model that systems should be easy to use and that designers should analyze the persuasion event to understand the user context.

In addition to system features, Vaghefi et al. [14] found characteristics of users themselves that made them more prone to IT addiction. In their study, a system's ease of use and its usefulness, among other features, were antecedents for IT addiction among users with certain characteristics. This postulate related to the impact of information scent and time constraints on users' stress, performance, and attitude [26]. Information scent is the collection of audio, visual, and semantic cues that guides users to the information they are seeking, making a system easy to use and positively influencing its performance.

The postulate stating that a system should be unobtrusive and should not disturb a user when s/he is performing a primary task arose in two of the studies, namely those by Cenfetelli and Schwarz [9] and Jenkins et al. [27]. The former [9] concerned six inhibitors that may prevent people from using a website. Among the inhibitors that had a negative consequence was intrusiveness, which was a quality of systems that interrupted users with unrequested tasks. Jenkins et al. [27] studied how interrupting a user

Table 1. Summary of effective system features and qualities categorized according to the PSD model [cf. 7]

PSD model		Negative effects	Mitigation effects
1. Persuasion postulates	Unobtrusiveness	–	System should not interrupt the user [9] Alert messages should not interrupt a user's primary task [27]
	Usefulness and ease of use	Usefulness and ease of use, among other related factors, were antecedents for addiction [14]	Systems that are complex and change often cause stress [8] Systems should not require too much effort or be deceptive [9] When a user feels the system will be useful and easy to use, their attitude toward it is positive [15] Systems should have the appropriate number of features for each type of user [25] Systems should guide a user to help them find relevant information [26] Performance failures should be avoided [28]
2. Persuasion context	Intent	–	–
	Event		Systems should fit into users' lives [8] A user's skills should be taken into account during system design [25] New technology should be well understood, before implementing in order to avoid failures [28] Systems should work as promised [31]
	Strategy	–	–
3. Persuasive system features	Primary task support	–	Parental monitoring may prevent addiction [10] Self-monitoring may decrease addiction [14]
	Computer–human dialogue	If systems are visually attractive, then they may be more addictive [14]	Education and suggestions may prevent addiction [10] Reminders and feedback may prevent addiction [14]
	Perceived credibility	–	–
	Social support	Social features may make systems more addictive [11, 10, 14, 29] Social facilitation may increase feelings of loneliness [30] Subjective norms regarding social networking site usage increase users' feelings of guilt and discontinuance intentions [32]	Recognition by others may decrease users' feelings of loneliness [30]

with security messages affected their secondary task. They found that if a user was performing a primary task when they were interrupted by the security message, then they often disregarded the message. Thus, the message not only interrupted users' primary tasks but also their secondary task (the security issue to which the message referred), which may be neglected.

Some studies in this review, namely [8, 9, 25, 27, 28], identified features that designers should avoid if they wish to increase the likelihood of system use. Maier et al. [8] identified and examined features that created social networking stress, which had a significant effect on individuals' intention to discontinue use of the system. Of the six features that created stress [8], some could be categorized using the PSD model, because they discussed the same issues as the postulate regarding ease of use and usefulness. For example, system features that created stress included the complexity and constant changes of social networking systems. The work of Cenfetelli and Schwarz [9] followed the same line. Tan, Benbasat, and Cenfetelli [28] found that e-service failures had a negative effect on customer expectations.

Another category that stood out from the results was social support. The features in this category often had negative consequences for IT users, for instance, they increased the addictive influence of IS (see, for instance, [10, 11, 29]) and increased feelings of loneliness [30]. Social features had a negative impact on users in all four studies that explored IT addiction from different perspectives. Social enhancement (the value of online social networks to users based on their perception of other members' acceptance and approval of them), envy (the emotion social network users feel when they desire the possessions or life experiences of other users), and a feeling of missing out on social events and announcements, also known as FOMO, which arises if users do not frequently monitor social networking systems) had significant effects on the addictive use of social networking sites [11].

In their study on addiction to mobile social applications, Kwon et al. [29] suggested that social applications are designed to increase social liquidity, which they defined as "the ease with which one can establish interpersonal relationships" but also as "the number of users available with whom social relationships can be cultivated." They concluded that when a person is more sensitive to social liquidity, s/he is more vulnerable to mobile social application addiction. Vaghefi et al. [14] found that some social support features affected an individual's tendency toward IT addiction, namely connectivity and access to all communication channels. In online gaming addiction, Xu et al. [10] recognized several social factors that increased addictive behavior, which were a need for relationships and system features that supported socializing.

Matook et al. [30] discovered that the type of social system feature could determine whether it had positive or negative influences on users' feelings of loneliness. Passive features, whereby users passively consume the content of other users, such as photos or status updates, increased their feelings of loneliness. In contrast, active social system features, whereby users broadcast their own content to friends and followers, decreased their feelings of loneliness.

We identified system features effective in mitigating the negative consequences of IT use also from other categories of the PSD model [7], namely event, primary task support, and dialogue support features. Event features were mainly concerned with knowing and understanding the use, user, and technology contexts. For example,

Saunders et al. [25] showed that systems designed to take different kinds of users into account, like those that provided a choice of basic or expert profiles, were less likely to cause stress. Vaghefi et al. [14] suggested that system features like usage reports (primary task support) and reminders (dialogue support) could help users to understand that their use of a system may not be totally under their control, which could mitigate its addictiveness.

In a case described by Salo and Frank [31], effects were more complicated. They studied the relationship between situational context and users' behavior after positive and negative critical incidents occurred with a mobile application. When a negative incident took place indoors, it led to negative word-of-mouth, which was not the case when it happened outdoors. When a negative incident occurred with a mobile application that had a physical aspect (that is, it required concrete interaction between the user and his/her mobile phone), users discontinued their system use more easily than after negative incidents relating to other kinds of systems. They concluded that systems should work as promised to prevent users from discontinuing their use. This fits with the PSD model's idea of understanding the technology context, especially as new technologies may not work as intended, which makes users more likely to stop using them.

5   Discussion

As the first postulate of the PSD model [7] states, IT is never neutral, as it will always influence users' behavior and attitudes in one way or another. This was evident in the findings of articles included in this review. Naturally, as we focused on articles about the dark side of IT use, effects on users were often negative. However, articles also revealed ways to mitigate negative consequences, although further studies are needed to investigate e.g. how changing context affects.

As a category, social features were clearly the most important in terms of causing negative consequences. They may cause, for example, stress, envy, addiction, feelings of loneliness, and other issues. In only one study were social features found to have a mitigating effect on a negative issue, which was users' feelings of loneliness. In general, social features can have many positive effects, for example, during health behavior change [33], but as this review shows, they also have a dark side. Social features should still be used in IT, but system designers should find ways to mitigate and prevent their negative effects. For example, it may be useful to remind users that one cannot see the whole picture of others' lives through IT.

The need for social features and how they are utilized should be considered carefully by software designers. In some systems, social features may be highly beneficial from a user's point of view, but this is not so in all cases. For example, a persuasive system supporting a user to become more active should be careful in sending repeated requests for the user to share their activities with others. It may well be that they do not wish to do so.

Multiple mitigating characteristics were found in our review. Most of them can be categorized within the postulates of the PSD model [7]. The postulate concerning a system's usefulness and ease of use came up most often among the studies we reviewed. This postulate is rather broad and covers many qualities of a good information system, so this finding was not very surprising. However, it was somewhat surprising that ideas relating to a system's ease of use and usefulness were still so dominant in the analyzed literature. In the IS field, these two concepts have been under investigation for decades, and their importance is clear. However, in practice, it still seems to be rather difficult to prevent systems from causing unnecessary negative consequences to users.

As mentioned above, five studies investigated negative qualities of systems that should be avoided in order to mitigate the negative consequences of IT use. If a system has errors, does not function as promised, or if it requires too much effort from users, their feelings toward the system are likely to be negative. In the modern era, with ever-increasing work and life demands on individuals and numerous information systems and applications available, there is no place for poorly functioning or excessively demanding systems in a leisure context.

If a system keeps changing its user interface without giving users enough time to adapt to the changes, they may stop using the system [8]. This finding is interesting, as it conflicts with the current trend of constantly modifying information systems. The frequency at which systems change, especially in relation to their user interfaces, should be carefully considered, as too many changes in a short period of time may cause users to leave rather than keeping them interested. Constant changes may cause stress, which may outweigh the benefits a system can deliver to users. This topic requires more research, especially in relation to different user groups.

Simplicity could be a good term to describe a system with few negative consequences for users. Systems should be easy for different kinds of users to learn and use. Depending on the system, there could be an option for users to choose different interfaces based on their skills; experienced users could use an advanced version offering a large number of features. Testing systems throughout the design and implementation phases and gathering feedback and use data from released systems could help to refine them to enhance the way they fit with users' lives.

Negative consequences of IT use can range from loss of productivity and stress [2, 3, 16] to depression and loneliness [14]. Minor negative consequences might constitute short-term negative feelings, such as annoyance or irritation, which may disappear by themselves over time. Although undesirable, it may be too costly to mitigate these kinds of minor negative consequences completely. Individuals are all different, so there is no way to create a system that would avoid causing negative emotions to every user.

However, major negative consequences that cause harm not just on the individual level but also on the societal level need special attention. Addiction to IT is one of the most severe negative consequences of IS use. In this analysis, features that mitigated IT addiction were usage monitoring and giving feedback. These features were suggested by authors and were not tested for effectiveness. The effectiveness of usage monitoring, whether by a parent, as in the case of adolescent gaming addictions [10], or in the form of self-monitoring, is an open issue that needs to be investigated in different settings. In any case, if users notice and think about their negative behavior early enough by self-monitoring and comparing their own use with that of others, then they could avoid addiction.

The analysis we have presented in this paper has some limitations. First, because our literature review included only studies from the basket of eight journals in the IS field, studies of the negative consequences of IT use outside of these journals were not analyzed. The number of articles we analyzed was therefore relatively low. However, the studies published in the journals we searched can be argued to represent the best research in the IS field. In addition, our review did not consider organizational contexts, which could be included in future studies to present a more complete picture of current research into features of IT use that mitigate its negative consequences. In spite of the limitations of this analysis, we were able to identify numerous gaps in knowledge in the studied area.

6 Conclusion

Information systems, regardless of their numerous benefits, also have negative effects on users and society. In this study, we analyzed previous research literature using the PSD model to identify system characteristics that could mitigate the negative effects of IT use. Most of the mitigating effects we identified in this review related to a system's usefulness and ease of use. In addition, systems that were unobtrusive and free from errors mitigated the negative consequences of IT use. Systems may cause negative feelings and consequences if they have many errors or if they are intrusive and disrupt users' primary tasks. Negative consequences of IT use can also be avoided or mitigated by understanding users and the context in which systems are used.

The features in the social support category were the primary cause of negative consequences in the studies we analyzed in this review. In some cases, they were found to cause, among other negative consequences, envy, loneliness, and addiction. However, in one dark side study, social features (that is, broadcasting to friends and followers) had a positive effect, as they reduced users' feelings of loneliness. Further research of social features in more specific contexts is needed to determine the further positive effects they might have on users and how they might mitigate the negative consequences of IT use. In one study in this review, reminders and self-monitoring were suggested as ways for users to avoid addiction to social networking applications.

The dark side of IT use is an issue that needs our attention. To find ways to mitigate the negative consequences of IT use, we first need to identify them. In this review, we compiled system characteristics from eight top IS journals that could mitigate the negative consequences of IT use. A system's ease of use and usefulness were valuable assets in this context. More research is needed to find other ways to mitigate the negative consequences of everyday IT use.

References

1. Oinas-Kukkonen, H., Oinas-Kukkonen, H.: Humanizing the Web: Change and Social Innovation. Palgrave Macmillan, Basingstoke (2013). https://doi.org/10.1057/978113730 5701
2. Tarafdar, M., Gupta, A., Turel, O.: Special issue on 'dark side of information technology use': an introduction and a framework for research. Inf. Syst. J. **25**(3), 161–170 (2015). https://doi.org/10.1111/isj.12070

3. Pirkkalainen H., Salo, M.: Two Decades of the Dark Side in the Information Systems Basket: Suggesting Five Areas for Future Research. In: Proceedings of the European Conference on Information Systems (ECIS) (2016)
4. Ragu-Nathan, T.S., Tarafdar, M., Ragu-Nathan, B.S., Tu, Q.: The consequences of technostress for end users in organizations: conceptual development and empirical validation. Inf. Syst. Res. **19**(4), 417–433 (2008). https://doi.org/10.1287/isre.1070.0165
5. Sapacz, M., Rockman, G., Clark, J.: Are we addicted to our cell phones? Comput. Hum. Behav. **57**, 153–159 (2016). https://doi.org/10.1016/j.chb.2015.12.004
6. Seo, H.A., Chun, H.Y., Jwa, S.H., Choi, M.H.: Relationship between young children's habitual computer use and influencing variables on socio-emotional development. Early Child. Dev. Care **181**(2), 245–265 (2011). https://doi.org/10.1080/03004430.2011.536644
7. Oinas-Kukkonen, H., Harjumaa, M.: Persuasive systems design: key issues, process model, and system features. Commun. Assoc. Inf. Syst. **24**(1), 485–500 (2009)
8. Maier, C., Laumer, S., Weinert, C., Weitzel, T.: The effects of technostress and switching stress on discontinued use of social networking services: a study of Facebook use. Inf. Syst. J. **25**(3), 275–308 (2015). https://doi.org/10.1111/isj.12068
9. Cenfetelli, R.T., Schwarz, A.: Identifying and testing the inhibitors of technology usage intentions. Inf. Syst. Res. **22**(4), 808–823 (2011). https://doi.org/10.1287/isre.1100.0295
10. Xu, Z., Turel, O., Yuan, Y.: Online game addiction among adolescents: motivation and prevention factors. Eur. J. Inf. Syst. **21**(3), 321–340 (2012). https://doi.org/10.1057/ejis.2011.56
11. James, T.L., Lowry, P.B., Wallace, L., Warkentin, M.: The effect of belongingness on obsessive-compulsive disorder in the use of online social networks. J. Manage. Inf. Syst. **34**(2), 560–596 (2017). https://doi.org/10.1080/07421222.2017.1334496
12. Turel, O., Qahri-Saremi, H.: Problematic use of social networking sites: antecedents and consequence from a dual-system theory perspective. J. Manage. Inf. Syst. **33**(4), 1087–1116 (2016). https://doi.org/10.1080/07421222.2016.1267529
13. Turel, O., Serenko, A., Giles, P.: Integrating technology addiction and use: an empirical investigation of online auction users. MIS Q. **35**(4), 1043–1061 (2011). https://doi.org/10.2307/41409972
14. Vaghefi, I., Lapointe, L., Boudreau-Pinsonneault, C.: A typology of user liability to IT addiction. Inf. Syst. J. **27**(2), 125–169 (2017). https://doi.org/10.1111/isj.12098
15. Pramatari, K., Theotokis, A.: Consumer acceptance of RFID-enabled services: a model of multiple attitudes, perceived system characteristics and individual traits. Eur. J. Inf. Syst. **18**(6), 541–552 (2009). https://doi.org/10.1057/ejis.2009.40
16. Tarafdar, M., D'Arcy, J., Turel, O., Gupta, A.: The dark side of information technology. MIT Sloan Manage. Rev. **56**(2), 60–70 (2015)
17. Karppinen, P., Oinas-Kukkonen, H.: Three approaches to ethical considerations in the design of behavior change support systems. In: Berkovsky, S., Freyne, J. (eds.) PERSUASIVE 2013. LNCS, vol. 7822, pp. 87–98. Springer, Heidelberg (2013). https://doi.org/10.1007/978-3-642-37157-8_12
18. Torning, K., Hall, C., Oinas-Kukkonen, H.: Persuasive system design: state of the art and future directions. In: Chatterjee, S., Parvati, D. (eds.) Fourth International Conference on Persuasive Technology, ACM International Conference, vol. 350, Article no. 30. ACM, New York
19. Karppinen, P., Oinas-Kukkonen, H., Alahäivälä, T., Jokelainen, T., Keränen, A.-M., Salonurmi, T., Savolainen, M.: Persuasive user experiences of a health behavior change support system: a 12-month study for prevention of metabolic syndrome. Int. J. Med. Inform. **96**, 51–61 (2016). https://doi.org/10.1016/j.ijmedinf.2016.02.005

20. Lehto, T., Oinas-Kukkonen, H.: Explaining and predicting perceived effectiveness and use continuance intention of a behaviour change support system for weight loss. Behav. Inf. Technol. **34**(2), 176–189 (2014). https://doi.org/10.1080/0144929X.2013.866162
21. Paré, G., Trudel, M.C., Jaana, M., Kitsiou, S.: Synthesizing information systems knowledge: a typology of literature reviews. Inf. Manage. **52**(2), 183–199 (2015). https://doi.org/10.1016/j.im.2014.08.008
22. Webster, J., Watson, R.T.: Analyzing the past to prepare for the future: writing a literature review. MIS Q. **26**(2), xiii–xxiii (2002)
23. Turel, O.: Quitting the use of a habituated hedonic information system: a theoretical model and empirical examination of Facebook users. Eur. J. Inf. Syst. **24**, 431–446 (2015). https://doi.org/10.1057/ejis.2014.19
24. Tams, S., Hill, K., Thatcher, J.: NeuroIS — alternative or complement to existing methods? Illustrating the holistic effects of neuroscience and self-reported data in the context of technostress research. J. Assoc. Inf. Syst. **15**(10), 723–753 (2014)
25. Saunders, C., Wiener, M., Klett, S., Sprenger, S.: The impact of mental representations on ICT-related overload in the use of mobile phones. J. Manage. Inf. Syst. **34**(3), 803–825 (2017). https://doi.org/10.1080/07421222.2017.1373010
26. Moody, G.D., Galletta, D.F.: Lost in cyberspace: the impact of information scent and time constraints on stress, performance, and attitudes online. J. Manage. Inf. Syst. **32**(1), 192–224 (2015). https://doi.org/10.1080/07421222.2015.1029391
27. Jenkins, J., Anderson, B., Vance, A., Kirwan, B., Eargle, D.: More harm than good? How messages that interrupt can make us vulnerable. Inf. Syst. Res. **27**(4), 880–896 (2016). https://doi.org/10.1287/isre.2016.0644
28. Tan, C.-W., Benbasat, I., Cenfetelli, R.T.: An exploratory study of the formation and impact of electronic service failures. MIS Q. **40**(1), 1–29 (2016). https://doi.org/10.25300/MISQ/2016/40.1.01
29. Kwon, H.E., So, H., Han, S.P., Oh, W.: Excessive dependence on mobile social apps: a rational addiction perspective. Inf. Syst. Res. **27**(4), 919–939 (2016). https://doi.org/10.1287/isre.2016.0658
30. Matook, S., Cummings, J., Bala, H.: Are you feeling lonely? the impact of relationship characteristics and online social network features on loneliness. J. Manage. Inf. Syst. **31**(4), 278–310 (2015). https://doi.org/10.1080/07421222.2014.1001282
31. Salo, M., Frank, L.: User behaviours after critical mobile application incidents: the relationship with situational context. Inf. Syst. J. **27**(1), 5–30 (2017). https://doi.org/10.1111/isj.12081
32. Turel, O.: Untangling the complex role of guilt in rational decisions to discontinue the use of a hedonic information system. Eur. J. Inf. Syst. **25**(5), 432–447 (2016). https://doi.org/10.1057/s41303-016-0002-5
33. Laranjo, L., Arguel, A., Neves, A.L., Gallagher, A.M., Kaplan, R., Mortimer, N., Mendes, G.A., Lau, A.Y.S.: The influence of social networking sites on health behavior change: a systematic review and meta-analysis. J. Am. Med. Inform. Assoc. **22**(1), 243–256 (2014). https://doi.org/10.1136/amiajnl-2014-002841

Combining Open and Closed Forms of Innovation: An Investigation of Emerging Tensions and Management Approaches

Emilie Ruiz[1] and Michela Beretta[2(✉)]

[1] Université Savoie-Mont-Blanc, 27 Rue Marcoz, 73000 Chambéry, France
[2] Aarhus University, Fuglesans Alle 4, 8000 Aarhus, Denmark
micbe@mgmt.au.dk

Abstract. It is increasingly common for firms to engage in both external and internal crowdsourcing to access ideas and solutions coming from external customers and internal employees. These IT platforms can be seen as forms of open and closed innovation search, where the first aims to perform distant search beyond the organizational boundaries, while the second is used to conduct local search within the firm. Nevertheless, limited attention has been placed on investigating which tensions emerge when firms combine these conflicting innovation search strategies and related management approaches to address them. By drawing on a qualitative, inductive case study of a large organization headquartered in France, our study identifies and discusses three key paradoxes emerging from pursuing both innovation forms: (1) paradox of identity; (2) paradox of organizing the innovation process; and (3) paradox of boundary management. Moreover, we discuss different management approaches implemented by managers to address the identified paradoxes.

Keywords: Crowdsourcing platforms · Paradoxes · Open innovation

1 Introduction

Open innovation has attracted the attention of both researchers and practitioners. The innovation management literature has focused on highlighting the benefits and costs of conducting open innovation activities, usually investigated in opposition to more closed innovation forms [1]. However, more recent studies point to the importance of going beyond the distinction between open vs. closed innovation to consider the notion of complex organizational boundaries [2]. That is, firms can combine both open and closed innovation search strategies to organize and support their innovation activities and access diverse inputs [2]. In fact, together with the reliance on external innovation sources, it is common for firms to engage in internal search practices for innovation to build on their existing domain knowledge [3].

A typical example is represented by the increasing implementation of external and internal crowdsourcing within the same firm to expand innovation search both within and beyond its organizational boundaries, spurred by the diffusion of new digital technologies [4]. Arguably, external and internal crowdsourcing can be regarded as,

© Springer International Publishing AG, part of Springer Nature 2018
S. D. Müller and J. A. Nielsen (Eds.): SCIS 2018, LNBIP 326, pp. 26–40, 2018.
https://doi.org/10.1007/978-3-319-96367-9_3

respectively, forms of open and closed innovation search. On the one hand, external crowdsourcing enables firms to perform a broader, distant search for ideas and solutions from a wider crowd of distributed actors outside the organizational boundaries [5]. On the other hand, internal crowdsourcing constitutes an internal search practice that enables firms to perform local search within the organizational boundaries by involving distributed employees in the innovation process [6].

However, engaging in open innovation activities is likely to create tensions with other internal search practices implemented within the organization for innovation purposes [7]. This is especially due to the fact that open and closed innovation forms are depicted by existing literature as being driven by inconsistent logics in terms of agency, control, motivation and locus of innovation [2]. These contrasting logics are likely to create substantial managerial and organizational challenges, making it more difficult for firms to combine them [8]. Relatedly, external and internal crowdsourcing initiatives are depicted by existing research as distinct innovation search forms - being characterized by a different locus of innovation, design requirements and type of targeted crowd [6]. As such, their combination may potentially create inherent tensions with respect to how to organize and manage the innovation process. This raises the question of how firms can simultaneously manage closed and open search activities and thus attend to both types of innovation logics [2]. Nevertheless, limited attention has been placed by current research on unfolding this important question.

Our study aims to contribute to this discussion by investigating which tensions emerge when firms combine open and closed innovation forms and corresponding management approaches to address them. In our study, this is exemplified by the simultaneous pursue of local and distant search activities through the combination of external and internal crowdsourcing. To this end, we draw on the paradox theory as a theoretical lens to shed more light on this aspect. This theory constitutes a relevant lens through which understand how firms manage contradictions [9] and has been used by various studies to explore complex tensions related to different organizational aspects, such as ambidexterity [10] and creativity [11].

In order to address our research question, we conducted an inductive, qualitative case study of a large French firm, which has attempted to combine open and closed innovation search through the implementation of both external and internal crowdsourcing, resulting in different challenges. By drawing on the paradox literature, we unfold the tensions that emerged when the firm pursued both innovation modes and the approaches managers implemented in the attempt to address them. More specifically, we identify and discuss paradoxes related to identity, the organization of innovation processes and boundary management, and find evidence of different management approaches based on integration, differentiation and acceptance strategies.

Our study contributes to current innovation literature in a number of ways. First, we extend recent calls on advancing a theory of the innovative firm that takes into account complex organizational boundaries where firms govern through a mix of contrasting innovation forms [2, 12]. Our findings offer an alternative framework for how firms manage open-closed innovation tensions, in this case related to the implementation of both external and internal crowdsourcing. By doing so, our study brings attention to the contradictory elements inherent in pursuing both distant and local innovation search strategies. Second, we integrate insights from the paradox literature as a way to reframe current discussion about open and closed innovation forms. We show how integrating the paradox lens enables to blend seemingly conflicting search strategies, thus highlighting the importance of seeing them as complementary rather than as polarized contradictions. Finally, our findings also have important implications for the information systems literature, where both internal and external crowdsourcing platforms have attracted the attention of various IS scholars over the last years [13, 14]. We provide more insights into the implementation of these online platforms in order to enable a better management.

2   Theoretical Background

2.1   Open and Closed Innovation Forms

Previous innovation studies have focused on contrasting open innovation with traditional 'proprietary' forms where internal employees generate ideas for new products, processes or services [1]. Increasing focus has been placed on addressing governance-related questions in the attempt to shed light on the benefits and costs of open and closed innovation forms. However, the open innovation literature often tends to examine open and closed innovation forms as strategic dilemmas or trade-offs – i.e. as choices that firms make between the two poles in order to organize for innovation [1]. Open and closed (internal) innovation are, in fact, often depicted as competing organizational modes for generating new knowledge and innovation. Different insights have been generated on the contingencies of these forms – i.e. when and under what conditions firms would benefit from conducting open innovation compared to closed (internal) innovation practices and vice versa [1, 5]. However, it is also recognized that such comparisons represent an idealized approach to facilitate theorization. In fact, firms are likely to organize and manage innovation through a more complex combination of internal and external search mechanisms [1, 2]. This is based on the insight that different types of sources of knowledge and ideas for innovation should be exploited, both within and outside the organizational boundaries.

In our study, we particularly zoom in on two forms of organizing for innovation: internal and external crowdsourcing. These platforms are enabled by information systems which provide the software and infrastructure to share ideas online [13]. While current research has shed light on the benefits and challenges of crowdsourcing, in this study we argue that combining these two search approaches is likely to generate tensions for the firm, arising from specific elements of these search strategies and underlying goals. We show how these tensions can be regarded as paradoxes, due to contradictory elements that need to be simultaneously managed by organization [15]. There are several reasons for the emergence of paradoxes when combining external and internal crowdsourcing, as highlighted below.

2.1.1   Locus of Innovation

Internal and external crowdsourcing enable firms to simultaneously involve two different types of crowds in the innovation process [16]. On the one hand, it is claimed that involving a large and diverse crowd of external contributors through crowdsourcing may be beneficial for the firm, due to the possibility to access both need-based and solution-based information [17]. On the other hand, many companies still tend to rely on internal expertise and knowledge bases to generate innovations [3]. Internal employees are often associated with domain-specific knowledge, accumulated through training and localized expertise that may be relevant for the generation of new ideas [18]. Moreover, they possess rich tacit knowledge about customers' needs and firms' products and processes as well as an in-depth understanding of the organizational context [19].

2.1.2 Type of Innovation Search

Relatedly, external and internal crowdsourcing can be regarded as having different starting points in the search for ideas and solutions. External crowdsourcing is implemented by firms with the aim to perform a distant search for ideas and solutions – i.e. going further away from the firm's current knowledge base [5]. However, it is also found that distant search creates challenges for firms in terms of absorptive capacity – i.e. of integrating and assimilating the inputs provided [20]. Moreover, this type of search bears the risk of loss of control for the firm, as it becomes more difficult to align contributors' ideation efforts with the organization's needs and strategies [6]. On the other hand, internal crowdsourcing enables firms to perform a broader local search spanning diverse boundaries within the organization, although still in the vicinity of the firm's current knowledge bases. Although local search decreases the probability of finding novel solutions, it increases the chances of identifying and integrating more feasible solutions [21].

2.1.3 Design Requirements

Current research highlights how in-bound open innovation tools like external crowdsourcing require firms to develop new practices and capabilities to favor the participation of external contributors and the integration of their inputs into the innovation processes [13]. One set of practices relates to the design of incentive mechanisms to support the involvement of external contributors and employees in innovation. These two types of crowds are likely to be driven by different motivations to participate in innovation activities, opening up the question of how firms can develop incentive systems that would align to the motivations of these crowds [16]. A second set of practices relates to the development of receiving mechanisms that enable the efficient processing, selection, transfer and integration of external and internal inputs. Considering the limited attentional capabilities of firms, a key question relates to how firms pay attention to and value the diverse knowledge generated through these different search processes [22]. In fact, it is found that managers are likely to value external and internal knowledge differently [22], an aspect that can have implications for how generated inputs may be filtered and processed. Moreover, current studies highlight the need for firms to establish new roles within the organization to enable the transfer and integration of externally generated ideas [23]. Involving internal and external crowds also require a different approach when it comes to managing intellectual property (IP) rights to the ideas and solutions generated [4].

2.2 A Paradox Lens

In this study, we draw on the paradox theory. Paradoxes are usually depicted as "contradictory yet interrelated elements that exist simultaneously and persist over time" [15, p. 382]. It is highlighted that managing paradoxes does not entail the elimination of emerging tensions, but rather it means to find ways to handle contradictory elements simultaneously [24]. Innovation literature highlights the existence of different paradoxes when it comes to the management of innovation processes. These paradoxes relate, for instance, to multiple identity demands for employees when engaging in creative activities [11, 25], the organization of innovation [10], learning [15], and the management of boundaries [26]. Research highlights that the act of organizing itself involves inherent contradictions due to the emergence of distinct roles and responsibilities as well as competing demands with respect to rules, structures and processes [15]. Building on this, paradox studies have discussed three main approaches to the management of tensions: (1) integration approaches which focus on embracing and leveraging the synergies between the opposing poles [10]; (2) differentiation approaches (spatial or temporal) which focus on splitting the two poles to leverage their distinct benefits [27, 28]; and (3) opposition approaches which entail the acceptance of the paradox [27]. We build on these insights to investigate which tensions emerge when firms combine both crowdsourcing models and related management approaches implemented to address them.

3 Method and Data

Our exploratory research entails a qualitative single case study based on data collected from a large French firm (labeled 'Gamma' for confidentiality reasons). Despite single case studies raise issues about the generalizability of the findings, they nevertheless are important to provide a more in-depth understanding and exploration of a phenomenon [29], in this case related to the emergence of tensions.

3.1 Research Setting

Gamma is a large French firm employing more than 30000 employees worldwide and leader in the small electric appliance market. In 2012, Gamma launched an internal collaborative platform in order to involve employees in innovation by encouraging the submission of unsolicited ideas and solutions to solve relevant technological problems. However, in 2016 the company decided to close this initiative due to a reorganization of the entire group. Over the years, the platform was not able to support the innovation process as initially intended. Yet, convinced by the value of internal collaborative innovation, Gamma decided to launch a new internal crowdsourcing platform in 2016 with the aim of collecting new ideas from the diverse crowd of distributed employees. Differently from the first internal crowdsourcing initiative, Gamma decided to organize the platform as being challenge-driven to support the innovation objective and increase employees' involvement. The new initiative was implemented with a specific process to support innovation: every year, based on an internal idea contest, the company planned to select five ideas on which to allocate funds to allow employees to further develop prototypes of selected ideas, ending with the selection of one final winner.

In 2014, Gamma also decided to create an external crowdsourcing platform on the impulsion of its Innovation Process Director, who believed in the importance of adopting open innovation practices. The objective of this platform was to enable the generation of new ideas and solutions by broadcasting complex problems that the firm was not able to solve to the crowd of external customers.

Hence, we selected Gamma for this exploratory, qualitative study because it constitutes a theoretically relevant context [30] to investigate emerging tensions and management approaches related to the combination of open (external) and closed (internal) innovation forms. In fact, the selected case represents a unique setting considering the aim of the firm to support and manage innovation through the use of two crowdsourcing platforms, thus shifting toward a dual innovation focus.

3.2 Data Collection

We collected our data through multiple sources. We conducted 18 semi-structured interviews with a number of different employees who were involved in the internal and/or external crowdsourcing platform. For instance, we interviewed managers involved in the management of both platforms and R&D teams in different business units, which were supposed to use both initiatives. We followed the suggestions provided by Andriopoulos and Lewis [10]: we did not use the terms paradoxes, contradictions or tensions during the interviews in order to not bias the interviewees and provide sufficient freedom in their answers. The interviews lasted between 20 and 186 min. All the interviews were recorded and fully transcribed in order to increase reliability [30].

In addition, we collected different secondary data sources. For instance, we collected various internal documents such as internal communication documents, reports, and presentations in order to fully understand the aim of each platform, the way both initiatives were implemented and managed, their performance and related challenges. We also organized two meetings in 2016 with various managers within Gamma. The aim of these meetings was to present preliminary findings to managers and gather their feedback and views on them as well as to generate further interpretations. These secondary data sources enabled to further augment and complement the insights emerging from the interview material.

3.3 Data Analysis

Our data analysis was conducted in an iterative manner and proceeded in different stages [31]. We conducted three rounds of coding using the Atlas.ti software. In the first stage, we read through the interview transcripts to identify relevant first-order concepts. We focused on categorizing underlying tensions as they were described by the interviewees. In the second stage, we aggregated the identified first-order concepts into second-order dimensions [31]. In the final stage, the identified dimensions were compared to detect patterns and relationships [31]. The resulting aggregated dimensions constituted the basis to develop our theoretical framework.

In particular, in order to label and refine the identified dimensions, we built on previous studies on paradoxes in innovation management [15]. This is because it was particularly evident from the interview material that interviewees were aware that combining both forms of innovation would determine the emergence of tensions. However, we noticed that such tensions were described by the interviewees not as either/or dilemmas or trade-offs but rather as paradoxes, being seen as complementary and valuable elements of innovation. Building on this, during the coding process we also focused on identifying which approaches managers implemented to address such tensions, by drawing on paradox studies. Table 1 provides an overview of the identified tensions and representative quotes.

Table 1. Representative quotes

Paradox	Underlying tensions	Representative quotes
Identity	Open vs closed values	"We tried the external platform, but it was not relevant. This idea of creating an internal community was because we have everything we need within the firm." (Research Manager)
	Specialization vs differentiation	"From a legal perspective, an employee who is out of his mission - who innovates on something that is not clearly depending on his business unit - is sanctioned on his salary. I know it can be a barrier for the internal challenge, where we encourage submission of ideas without business unit frontiers…but maybe it can help someone who wants to be open." (Lab employee, internal challenge manager)
Organizing the innovation process	Collaboration vs competition Control vs flexibility	"A challenge with competition mode is gratifying, stimulating. Challengers will outperform. (…) It is individual-based because we want all employees, even from purchasing or accountability, to participate. Teams would have encouraged R&D focus." (Lab employee, internal challenge manager)
Boundary management	Internal vs external knowledge	"Between the KPIs that pressure us to use external knowledge and all actions supporting valuation of our own knowledge, we don't know where to go." (Project leader)

4   Findings

4.1   Paradox of Identity: Conflicting Employee Roles

"On the one hand, you have to be open to innovate with external stakeholders…but on the other hand, you have to do it internally. This is quite confusing…" (Project leader)

Underlying Tensions. Combining both external and internal crowdsourcing initiatives created tensions of multiple identity demands [11] for employees, as they were required to be open (externally-focused) and closed (internally-focused) at the same time. On the one hand, by opening the organizational boundaries to the external crowd, the firm aimed to encourage employees to be open and innovate with external unidentified stakeholders [2]. In this case, R&D employees were required to shift their identity from problem solvers to solution seekers [25], broadcasting challenges to the external crowd. On the other hand, by focusing on internal crowdsourcing, employees were encouraged by the firm to innovate internally and to contribute to the organization as idea creators and problem-solvers. This emphasis on both *open and closed values* contributed to create ambiguity in identity work for employees. Potentially conflicting identities may especially emerge when employees need to internalize different role expectations [11]. In our case, conflicting identities emanated from employees' need to assume opposing but coexisting roles and memberships (related to both platforms) creating ambiguity and confusion about what they were supposed to do. Our interviewees highlighted that such ambiguity lead to a lack of interest and involvement in using both platforms over time, as they were trying to satisfy both competing demands.

Another aspect emerging from our analysis related to the underlying tension faced by employees in terms of adhering to the competing demands of *specialization and differentiation.* The company has particularly supported over the years the specialization of its employees when it comes to the conduction of work activities. Working contracts typically specify the activities and tasks employees are supposed to conduct, an aspect that limits their autonomy and freedom to engage in extra-role behaviors. In the context of the external crowdsourcing platform, this employee's specialization was valued and supported by the firm. When the innovation manager received an idea through the external platform, great attention was provided in identifying the right internal organizational members for its further development: *"We have to identify carefully who will be involved with the external user to be sure that the idea has all the chances to be integrated"* (Innovation Process Director). In this case, employees were required to focus on their area of expertise when collaborating with external actors to further develop their ideas.

However, this focus on specialization was in contrast with the way the internal crowdsourcing platform aimed to involve employees. In this case, it was considered important that employees would go beyond their expected roles and responsibilities when engaging in innovation, thus seeking ideas and solutions in new knowledge areas. This somehow required a shift in the professional identity of employees to embrace new roles directed at applying their knowledge and skills in less familiar areas as well as at engaging in creative efforts outside their particular knowledge comfort zone.

Management Approaches. We found that, in order to address the identified tensions related to identity, managers resorted to a mixed approach. On the one hand, they resorted to an acceptance approach, with the aim to appreciate tensions' differences and use them constructively [27]. It is important to point out that managers did not simply ignore this paradox. However, as reported by the Research Director, it seemed difficult to conciliate both open and closed values as well as specialization and differentiation roles for employees when innovating. As such, acceptance led somehow to a view of the paradox as unsolvable and persistent [15]. We noticed that the organization particularly aimed to develop over time an organizational culture based on this rich identity that would embrace both types of roles and values. At the same time, the firm considered it important to not rush in changing the culture in order to find the right balance to juxtapose the identity tensions. This entailed being clear and transparent with its employees in the attempt to reduce confusions and frustrations related to the identified competing demands. For instance, communication tactics aimed to emphasize organizational values that linked both types of identities to improve fit with organizational expectations, in the attempt to drive a cultural change. Moreover, when the second internal crowdsourcing initiative was introduced subsequently to the failure of the previous one, the firm decided to adopt a differentiation (spatial) approach [28] in order to separate the management of such platform from the external one. While the two platforms were initially managed within the Innovation Process Team at the corporate building, Gamma decided to separate the management of the new internal platform from the external one by assigning it to the internal Fab Lab unit, which was located in a separate building. This spatial separation was considered important to support and enable a better understanding of the distinct employees' roles.

4.2   Paradox of Organizing the Innovation Process

"It is disturbing to be so structured when using the external crowdsourcing platform and so flexible when using the internal crowdsourcing platform. It is just like doing the splits, the innovation splits." (Research project manager)

Underlying Tensions. Our interviewees highlighted that the implementation of both initiatives created contrasting demands for employees in terms of *collaborating and competing* among each other. On the one hand, one of the key aspects supporting the implementation of the external crowdsourcing platform related to fostering the involvement of and collaboration between cross-functional teams. Employees were thus strongly encouraged by the firm to work together and collaborate to support the development and integration of external ideas. On the other hand, the first internal crowdsourcing platform was designed to foster competition among employees. Differently from the external platform, the second internal initiative required employees to work individually while not supporting team-based collaboration. Implementing both initiatives also determined different ways of organizing – i.e. competing demands between *control and flexibility*. On the one hand, the external crowdsourcing platform was implemented with a structured process, where the firm aimed to exercise a high level of control on how employees could use the platform to support innovation and integrate external knowledge with internal innovation processes and activities. These processes and control were considered important to encourage employees to use the platform in the intended way.

On the contrary, when implementing the internal crowdsourcing platform, the firm regarded it as crucial to provide employees with the flexibility and freedom necessary to innovate in order to engage them in such initiative. This flexibility entailed, for instance, free access to the Lab, flexible time during working hours to dedicate to innovation and creativity and lack of a process to follow when doing so. As explained by the manager in charge of the challenge, *"If we want the challenge to work, we need to let them [participants] be free, to manage them differently. We stay open on this aspect."*

Negative Consequences. We found that these contrasting demands created an uncomfortable, even hostile environment for employees. While employees were encouraged to be collaborative when using both the first internal crowdsourcing platform and the external one, the use of competition-driven challenges for the newer internal initiative led to confusion. As these platforms were meant to be complementary, employees could face situations in which they had to collaborate with other colleagues when using the external crowdsourcing platform to integrate external ideas, while having to compete with the same colleagues during the internal challenge. Moreover, the encouragement of using both platforms led to feelings of overload and confusion for employees, as these initiatives were driven by different rules, structures and workflows which required employees to exert more efforts to engage in them. The discomfort and confusion of the situation led employees to lose interest in both initiatives: *"I don't want to use these platforms anymore, this is too complicated: I just want to do my job."* (Project leader).

Management Approaches. We found that, in order to manage these organizing tensions, the firm resorted to both spatial and temporal differentiation [28]. In relation to spatial separation, the firm decided that the two initiatives would be managed separately and assigned to different units as a way to reduce employee confusion. The aim was to communicate more clearly to employees that the internal crowdsourcing platform was managed by a different entity, by a different manager and in a different place - while at the same time maintaining some level of integration: *"When the new headquarter was built, it has been a real question: did we have to be integrated or stay aside? Being integrated seemed to be the better solution to attract people. However, as you can see, despite our integration, we have a dedicated building, separate from corporate."* (*Internal challenge manager*). In addition to this, managers resorted to temporal differentiation as a way to ease the underlying tensions. This means that employee participation to these initiatives was seen as a sequence of events [27], meaning that employees could dedicate specific times to each platform, thus switching between them.

4.3 Paradox of Boundary Management: Valuing Internal vs. External Knowledge

This boundary paradox relates to the combination of external and internal knowledge flows to feed the innovation process [26].

Underlying Tensions. Our interviewees highlighted that the use of both initiatives created confusion for managers with regards to the evaluation of internal and external knowledge. The external platform was implemented with the clear goal of accessing valuable, external knowledge residing outside the firm. R&D employees were then assigned the responsibility to identify, absorb and exploit such knowledge. The fact that external, distant knowledge was highly valued can also be seen in the implementation of KPIs from top management to measure the performance of the external platform and its contribution to the innovation process. Employees were thus encouraged to value external knowledge. The external crowdsourcing platform, however, conflicted with employees' expectations that their own ideas generated through the internal platform would be considered by the firm. In this case, the internal initiative was implemented with the ultimate goal to exploit internal knowledge residing across the whole organization to innovate. As such, this initiative encouraged employees to support and value internal knowledge, somehow reinforcing the NIH (Not-Invented-Here) mindset that still many employees had. Hence, the pressure from top management to value external knowledge while at the same time having to exploit internal knowledge in the innovation process created confusion for employees in terms of how to allocate attention to both types of knowledge and how to capture value from both.

"Between the KPIs that pressure us to use external knowledge and all actions supporting valuation of our own knowledge, we don't know where to go." (Project leader)

Besides, when focusing on the external platform, managers faced a challenge related to the integration of external knowledge with the firm's internal knowledge bases. In contrast, internal knowledge generation, building on existing knowledge bases, was seen as easier to integrate and assimilate into current practices and activities. In fact, our interviewees highlighted that the ideas submitted to the internal crowdsourcing platforms were more likely to be implemented compared to the ideas identified through the external platform. Such preference for internal knowledge was also evident in the belief of many R&D employees that challenges did not necessarily have to be broadcasted outside the organizational boundaries, as internal employees possessed the right knowledge and expertise to address them: *"Why would I ask the crowd? My colleagues and I know our job; we don't need to ask people who don't know anything about our job". (Research Director).*

Negative Consequences. We found that this unbalance between the use of internal and external knowledge led to various negative consequences, not only for R&D employees but also for managers and higher-level management. For instance, top managers strongly supported the use of the external crowdsourcing platform, which was instead somehow avoided by employees. Moreover, while top management strongly encouraged employees to use the external platform, actions were not taken in case employees did not use it. This led top managers to lose credibility in the eyes of employees. This also affected the manager in charge of the external crowdsourcing platform, who lost the motivation to manage the platform and dedicate efforts in engaging people.

Management Approaches. In the attempt to manage such tension, the firm decided to reorganize knowledge flows to conciliate both internal and external knowledge creation activities and reduce ambiguities. In order to do so, they resorted to an integration approach [28] directed at leveraging synergies between the two search strategies. For instance, when developing the new version of the internal platform, the firm decided to implement a new IT tool for internal communication. This system allowed the firm to integrate the external and internal platform by using the same IT system. By doing so, it was possible to link and more easily integrate innovation-related news, shared projects, data about generated ideas and other types of information coming from both platforms. This was seen as a way to create synergy between all the generated knowledge, whether internal or external: *"It is much simpler to use [the IT tool]. We can communicate, access data extracted from both crowdsourcing platforms and I think they want to support us to use all this knowledge." (Research manager).*

However, conciliating both types of knowledge is still considered challenging by the firm, which aims to implement new practices and processes in the future in the attempt to combine both approaches.

5 Discussion

In this study, we aimed to shed more light on the tensions emerging when combining external and internal crowdsourcing and management approaches to address them. Our study provides a number of contributions to the innovation management literature. First, our study addresses recent calls related to the need to go beyond the distinction between open and closed innovation processes to investigate complex organizational boundaries [2, 7]. It is claimed that theories of innovation should be enriched by an exploration of the tensions emerging when dealing with contrasting innovation modes, especially considering that the firm-centered (internal) innovation logic differs from the open innovation one [2]. We extend these studies by providing a better understanding of the tensions and challenges emerging when firms attempt to combine external and internal crowdsourcing initiatives.

By integrating insights from the paradox theory, a second contribution of our study to current literature is to reframe the discussion about open and closed innovation. We show how the integration of this theory enables to develop a richer understanding of seemingly contradictory innovation search strategies, highlighting the importance of seeing them as complementary rather than as either/or dilemmas. In fact, when studying how to organize for innovation in the context of open vs. closed innovation forms, a typical approach used by previous research is represented by the contingency perspective [1, 12]. However, it is claimed that a key issue with such an approach is that it limits the focus on a limited number of variables, while oversimplifying contexts that are often more complex and dynamic [15]. Our study adopts a different approach and builds on the paradox literature to investigate how firms can engage in and attend to different types of external and internal innovation forms. We thus shift the focus of attention from choosing between different, contrasting innovation search modes to embracing their contradictions. We provide a complementary view on open and closed forms of innovation that extends current innovation research.

Relatedly, our study contributes to the paradox literature by extending its application to open and closed innovation forms. While the paradox theory has been used as a theoretical lens by various studies to shed light on tensions emerging when organizing for innovation [10, 15] as well as when fostering creativity in organizations [11], this lens seldom is employed to understand aspects related to innovation search and management within and across organizational boundaries.

A third contribution of our study to innovation literature relates to the role of identity in innovation, an aspect that has been understudied when it comes to innovation processes [25, 32]. Our findings show how combining both innovation modes can led to the emergence of identity threats, as R&D employees working at the boundary of the organization face the challenge of having to cope with multiple roles (being both solution seekers and problem solvers) and innovation values (promoting both open and closeness). We shed light on which management approaches managers implemented in the attempt to address such identity threats. In this respect, studies on creativity tensions highlight the creation of a meta-identity [11] as a potential integration approach to embrace multiple identity demands and mitigate ambiguity. It focuses on reconciling identity tensions by leveraging their interdependencies. In our case, the aim of the firm to build an organizational culture which embraces both values and multiple roles may be seen as a way contribute to the development of such superordinate identity over time, potentially leading employees to appreciate both internal and external knowledge.

Our findings also contribute to crowdsourcing research, by shedding more light on paradoxes related to the organization of innovation processes and boundary management. In relation to the organization of innovation processes, the study provides more insights into the competing demands of collaboration and competition as well as of flexibility and control, which emerge when designing these crowdsourcing platforms. These aspects related to the design have been, however, not thoroughly investigated [13]. In relation to the paradox of boundary management, previous research highlights that, when managers face the task of valuing internal and external knowledge, they tend to have a preference for outsiders [22]. Our findings seem to show a different picture which more closely aligns with the NIH syndrome highlighted by various studies [33], which leads organizational members to value the knowledge generated internally as superior to knowledge that lies outside the organizational boundaries.

Finally, our findings have important implications for IS research, which has recently started to investigate the design of internal and external crowdsourcing platforms for innovation [4, 14]. We shed light on the challenges and tensions emerging when firms attempt to combine both crowdsourcing models.

6 Conclusions

By drawing on the paradox theory, this study focused on investigating the tensions emerging when firms combine internal and external crowdsourcing and related management approaches. Future research could investigate whether the identified tensions and management approaches extend to other settings. Moreover, our analysis focused on internal and external crowdsourcing as two innovation search strategies that are open (external) and closed (internal). It could be interesting to extend the investigation of tensions and management approaches to other innovation forms employed by firms to exploit both internal and external knowledge.

References

1. Felin, T., Zenger, T.R.: Closed or open innovation? Problem solving and the governance choice. Res. Policy **43**(5), 914–925 (2014)
2. Lakhani, K.R., Lifshitz-Assaf, H., Tushman, M.: Open innovation and organizational boundaries: task decomposition, knowledge distribution and the locus of innovation. In: Handbook of Economic Organization: Integrating Economic and Organizational Theory, pp. 355–382 (2013)
3. Laursen, K.: Keep searching and you'll find: what do we know about variety creation through firms' search activities for innovation? Ind. Corp. Change **21**(5), 1181–1220 (2012)
4. Birkinshaw, J., Bouquet, C., Barsoux, J.L.: The 5 myths of innovation. MIT Sloan Manage. Rev. **52**(2), 43–50 (2011)
5. Afuah, A., Tucci, C.L.: Crowdsourcing as a solution to distant search. Acad. Manage. Rev. **37**(3), 355–375 (2012)
6. Zuchowski, O., et al.: Internal crowdsourcing: conceptual framework, structured review, and research agenda. J. Inf. Technol. **31**(2), 166–184 (2016)
7. Dahlander, L., Gann, D.M.: How open is innovation? Res. Policy **39**(6), 699–709 (2010)
8. Tushman, M., Lakhani, K.R., Lifshitz-Assaf, H.: Open innovation and organization design (2012)
9. Smith, W.K., Tushman, M.L.: Managing strategic contradictions: a top management model for managing innovation streams. Organ. Sci. **16**(5), 522–536 (2005)
10. Andriopoulos, C., Lewis, M.W.: Exploitation-exploration tensions and organizational ambidexterity: managing paradoxes of innovation. Organ. Sci. **20**(4), 696–717 (2009)
11. Gotsi, M., et al.: Managing creatives: paradoxical approaches to identity regulation. Hum. Relat. **63**(6), 781–805 (2010)
12. Nickerson, J.A., Zenger, T.R.: A knowledge-based theory of the firm—the problem-solving perspective. Organ. Sci. **15**(6), 617–632 (2004)
13. Majchrzak, A., Malhotra, A.: Towards an information systems perspective and research agenda on crowdsourcing for innovation. J. Strateg. Inf. Syst. **22**(4), 257–268 (2013)
14. Malhotra, A., et al.: Developing innovative solutions through internal crowdsourcing. MIT Sloan Manage. Rev. **58**(4), 73 (2017)
15. Smith, W.K., Lewis, M.W.: Toward a theory of paradox: a dynamic equilibrium model of organizing. Acad. Manage. Rev. **36**(2), 381–403 (2011)
16. Erickson, L., Petrick, I., Trauth, E.: Hanging with the right crowd: matching crowdsourcing need to crowd characteristics (2012)
17. Piller, F.T., Walcher, D.: Toolkits for idea competitions: a novel method to integrate users in new product development. R&D Manage. **36**(3), 307–318 (2006)
18. Unsworth, K.L., Parker, S.: Proactivity and innovation: promoting a new workforce for the new workplace. In: Holman, D.A.W., Toby, D., Clegg, C.W., Sparrow, P., Howard, A. (eds.) The New Workplace: A Guide to the Human Impact of Modern Working Practices, pp. 175–196. Wiley, Chichester (2003)
19. Simula, H., Ahola, T.: A network perspective on idea and innovation crowdsourcing in industrial firms. Ind. Mark. Manage. **43**(3), 400–408 (2014)
20. Cohen, W.M., Levinthal, D.A.: Absorptive-capacity - a new perspective on learning and innovation. Adm. Sci. Q. **35**(1), 128–152 (1990)
21. Poetz, M.K., Schreier, M.: The value of crowdsourcing: can users really compete with professionals in generating new product ideas? J. Prod. Innov. Manage **29**(2), 245–256 (2012)

22. Menon, T., Pfeffer, J.: Valuing internal vs. external knowledge: explaining the preference for outsiders. Manage. Sci. **49**(4), 497–513 (2003)
23. Whelan, E., et al.: Creating employee networks that deliver open innovation. MIT Sloan Manage. Rev. **53**(1), 37–44 (2011)
24. Oinonen, M., et al.: In search of paradox management capability in supplier–customer co-development. Industrial Marketing Management (2017)
25. Lifshitz-Assaf, H.: Dismantling knowledge boundaries at NASA: from problem solvers to solution seekers (2016)
26. Gebert, D., Boerner, S., Kearney, E.: Fostering team innovation: why is it important to combine opposing action strategies? Organ. Sci. **21**(3), 593–608 (2010)
27. Poole, M.S., Van de Ven, A.H.: Using paradox to build management and organization theories. Acad. Manage. Rev. **14**(4), 562–578 (1989)
28. Lewis, M.W.: Exploring paradox: toward a more comprehensive guide. Acad. Manage. Rev. **25**(4), 760–776 (2000)
29. Yin, R.K.: Case Study Research: Design and Methods. SAGE Publications, Beverly Hills (2009)
30. Eisenhardt, K.M.: Building theories from case-study research. Acad. Manage. Rev. **14**(4), 532–550 (1989)
31. Miles, M.B., Huberman, A.M.: Qualitative Data Analysis: An Expanded Sourcebook. SAGE Publications, Thousand Oaks (1994)
32. Bogers, M., et al.: The open innovation research landscape: established perspectives and emerging themes across different levels of analysis. Ind. Innov. **24**(1), 8–40 (2017)
33. Katz, R., Allen, T.J.: Investigating the Not Invented Here (NIH) syndrome: a look at the performance, tenure, and communication patterns of 50 R & D project groups. R&D Manage. **12**(1), 7–20 (1982)

Business Process Management, Continuous Improvement and Enterprise Architecture: In the Jungle of Governance

Torben Tambo[1](✉) ⓘ and Nikolaj Dybdal Clausen[2]

[1] Aarhus University, Birk Centerpark 15, 7400 Herning, Denmark
torbento@btech.au.dk
[2] 7400 Herning, Denmark

Abstract. Business Process Management (BPM) is fundamental in IT/IS systems requirement specifications and is also well positioned in Enterprise Architecture (EA) frameworks and practices. Continuous Improvement (CI) relates to agendas of lean, six sigma, and incessant push for increased effectiveness of the organization. This paper is developing a position of EA-driven BPM as being long-term, strategic and "slow", whereas CI is short-term, operational and "fast". A case study is presented, where CI is furthermore locally based and BPM is centrally based in a larger organization. This leads to conflicts between BPM and CI where the corporate value of both is eroded as IS initiatives on ERP implementation are prolonged and CI initiatives fail to match to-be scenarios. This paper discuss EA as a mediator, where EA is communicating business opportunities to "positive" CI initiatives and aiming at stopping "negative" CI initiatives. An EA-based process tracing mechanism is suggested and demonstrated connecting business processes, ERP, and silo-based elements for CI initiatives. Furthermore, a CI project management tool is discussed to outline screening opportunities for EA-based CI reviews. An agenda is developed to ensure that CI projects are developed according to the Enterprise Architecture and developed along the organizational architecture and not as silo projects. Furthermore Enterprise Architecture is in such case not alone to induce changes and EA must develop methods to synchronise and coordinate with other change processes.

Keywords: Enterprise Architecture · Business Process Management
Continuous Improvement

1 Introduction

Business Process Management (BPM) is a commonplace regime for structuration of work processes in information systems (IS) [1]. BPM is widely accepted for use in requirements engineering, formalization of work process narratives and human-computer interface descriptions. Enterprise Architecture (EA) describes the relationship

---

N. D. Clausen—Business Architect.

© Springer International Publishing AG, part of Springer Nature 2018
S. D. Müller and J. A. Nielsen (Eds.): SCIS 2018, LNBIP 326, pp. 41–54, 2018.
https://doi.org/10.1007/978-3-319-96367-9_4

between business strategy and technology; BPM is one of several artefacts of EA [2–5]. EA and BPM forms the corporate trajectory from as-is to to-be states; as this is often requiring larger scale systems engineering and change management its time dimension is extensive. Continuous Improvement (CI) is likewise commonly accepted in corporate governance in order to adapt to rapid changes, and create short-term transitional initiatives overcoming here-and-now deficiencies related to operational efficiency, market requirements, manufacturing circumstances or legislative issues [6–8]. This is not overlooking that CI is often and foremost a management philosophy linking to especially lean thinking.

Looking at CI as the fast track of decision-making and implementation of change this paper is analyzing and discussing the relationship between EA, BPM and CI as contradictory and sometimes counter-productive. The lens of the paper is that EA most obvious as a potential mediating factor. We claim that changes affecting any form of architecture – also from other management systems - must be governed within EA to maintain the best possible (digital) representation of the link between business strategy and the operating model. The research question is stated as: Can EA embrace CI to a level where benefits of CI in terms of value and speed is integrated into the BPM, or will CI run disjointly with BPM and blur the EA with reduced value as a consequence?

This paper is based on a case study from the company Delight Inc. Delight operates both an EA and a CI program. The associated with the EA program resides a BPM program that is managed centrally for ensuring alignment between business process and the ERP system. The CI programme is mostly managed decentrally. The CI programme is largely assumed to impact the BPM program negatively, and a more explicit EA implementation effort is review to ensure value creation.

2 Methodology

The methodology for the paper is twofold; a systematic literature review (SLR) from Kitchenham and Charters [9] and a qualitative, interpretive case study from Saunders [10] and Walsham [11]. The case study was performed during 2016–17 through interviews, action research and observations in Delight. The case study provided an understanding of the literature in context to a case in order to acquire practical knowledge within the paper topics [10]. The literature review is based on the SLR framework [9]; Planning, execution and analysis. This method is chosen to have a clearly define methodology for the literature review and SLR is a well-defined methodology as a framework for a literature review [9].

The literature review has been conducted from different sources in the reviewing process to identify relevant literature for the research. A broad range of general scientific search databases has been used, a.o. IEEE, ScienceDirect, SpringerLink and Google Scholar.

Predefined keywords have been identified based on the research questions. The keywords relevant to search in these sources to identify relevant knowledge for the research questions. The keywords have been used to identify relevant articles by searching the keywords in the paper's metadata. EA, CI and BPM easily yields relevant results, however the intersection between the concepts is less easy especially when it comes to a critical analysis of the interrelations. A number of papers are included where a general critical posture to the concepts of EA and CI is presented. This position is introduced to understand the theoretical motivation for a gap between EA and CI.

The action research took place by posting a BPM/EA specialist (co-author) from the global headquarter in the largest European sales offices for 3 months. The research is a part of an overall longitudinal study in the company initiated in 2014 and remains ongoing. The specialist reviewed recent (local) CI initiatives, and added these to a database of local initiatives. Also was made open presentations of the (central) BPM program as organizational interventions. Mock-ups and basic training were made to elicit further knowledge on motives and drivers, and incite user responses on viability of CI initiatives in the light of the BPM program. With a final aim of defining solutions to improve governance, improve IS project success, and elevate awareness in the organization, the study furthermore has elements of pragmatism [12] and design science [13].

3 Theory and Background

EA is the "analysis and documentation of an enterprise in its current and future states from an integrated strategy, business, and technology perspective" [14]. Its quintessence lies in building an organizing meta-context for an alignment of technology planning, and business planning to its strategic planning as its primary driver [5, 14]. EA defines the policies and standards for design of technologies, databases and application to the business. The role of Enterprise Architect is to strategically organise and design the technology components to aim for strategic alignment [14]. Lankhorst [5] defines EA as instrumental for the integration of business and technology across the organization consisting of four fundamental elements; "organizational structure, business processes, information systems and infrastructure" [5].

EA is about "planning, design, and integration activities related to a company's business processes, information and technology infrastructure" [15] holistic but related to: System information, applications, technical and business units; EA needs to considered as a framework that help to control direction and effort [1].

EA is about relationships and elements of the business and the tool to integrate, govern and analyze the organizational elements [16]. Bernus [2] describes these elements as a complex system that EA should be designed for organizational performance. EA is instrumental in analyzing grap between the current state and future state architecture [4]. Shuja [17] describes EA's role to identify the gap between as-is and to-be architecture and EA to ensure proper linkages. Pontacoloni [18] has defined the roles of an Enterprise Architect as to have understanding and overview of the entire enterprise, both internal and external.

The goals for EA is to be able to identify the above incompatible systems, e.g. Feral Information Systems [27], and integrate them in the organizational architecture. EA should be able to identify changes in the business and identify the challenges that will affect the business [13]. Rouhani [28] focuses on effective communication across the teams with process maps as enablers to communicate, coordinate and cooperate.

von Rosing et al. [29] describes BPM as a management process entailing work practices, life-cycle of actions, and structuration of services. von Rosing finds EA as the technology discipline that sets the framework for the business design. Witts separates BPM and EA stating that BPM is to capture and improve the business processes to achieve efficiency [30].

Bernus [2] do not see the benefits acquired in EA, if the documentation of the business processes does not meet quality standards. BPM provides the methods and tools in order for the organization to manage and optimize the processes [31]. BPM is to achieve process efficiency, process compliance, process standardization, process agility and process visibility [31]. The Process Architecture of EA can apply value and create the holistic overview of the processes [32]. As Schooff [32] describes leads BPM to Business Architecture which lead to Enterprise Architecture. The value created with EA is reflected by how the organization manage the business processes of the EA architecture layer, the business architecture and fit into the architecture [29]. von Rosing [29] add visual modelling of EA to Lankhorsts perspective [5]. Bernus [2] correlates EA standards with ISO9001, which requires that the business processes are modelled and shared across the enterprise.

Aligning BPM and EA can be a helpful tool in order to define the interoperability in services, e.g. applications in the organization [33]. Aligning the business processes with the Application and Technology architecture will create added value in the organization [29]. According to von Rosing et al. [29] can neither BPM nor EA stand alone as the people of EA focuses on IT alignment and the people of BPM focuses on business optimization, efficiency, effectiveness through CI.

With a focus on CI, the EA elements need to be integrated into the projects. In a project, the focus shall not only be on improving the process, but also take into consideration the data, technologies and services [14]. Rouhani [28] supports the project view with 8-step model for running projects: Identification; Conceptualization; Requirements definition; Design; Implementation description; Construction; Operation; Decommission.

EA management plans must be seen as improvement projects from a holistic view [3]. Achieving the alignment between BPM and EA will create transparency across the organization [29]. EA will ensure that BPM have data to perform performance measure and additionally have the agility to change business processes [29]. Finally, both BPM and EA covers the Enterprise Landscape and the combination will provide a better outcome and achieve strategic alignment across the organization [4].

In order to achieve agility, BPM must support CI in the organization [29]. Lankhorst [5] indicates that CI must address the EA and not the BPM. CI programs are based on process lifecycles, where BPM will set the desired changes and EA will align with the future state by changing the enterprise architecture accordingly [29, 33]. It is the responsibility for the Enterprise Architect to be able to achieve sufficient adaptability of all the EA layers [1] and achieve more flexibility that complexity [29].

As governance frameworks, EA and CI are forming a mainstream within their respective fields, however EA and CI are also subject to criticism. EA is stated as a (relatively) young discipline, with van Steenbergen et al. [19] proposing a multi-criteria maturity model where companies and architects can be low on maturity leading to failure as well as high on a sufficient range of criteria leading to successful transformation. EA – read as Enterprise Engineering – is criticized by Dietz et al. [20] for being based on the principles from scientific management and overlooking complexity and human dimensions. Congruent findings are obtained by Hope et al. [21] in pinpointing EA implementation as (risk of) failing to capture practice, routines and improvisations. Seppannen [22] presents a set of critical success factors for EA to balance between the pressure for (digital) enterprise transformations and the organisations capability, readiness and receptiveness to an architectural mindset.

CI is criticized for its short term goal-race insufficiently creating sustained result [23]. McCann et al. [24] has researched lean management and CI and found significant problems in having CI produce lasting impacts; over time impact erodes. The explanatory framework is related to CI claiming impact is areas where other governance regimes set minimum standards, or where employees feel stronger commitment to professional practices than to "management fads" [25].

The dual strands of governance outlined by CI and EA is presented in Fig. 1. The mutual influence is illustrated in the figure as counting aspects ranging from business strategy to influence on the operating model of the company. A critical gap is represented by the uncoordinated change of business processes [26, 27]. The gap is constituted by factors like (1) EA involves technology, CI is not necessarily involving technology, (2) architecture can be a purpose of its own in EA, CI is to deliver immediate business results, (3) EA is founded in long-term orientation, CI is fundamentally short-term oriented. The latter gap factor is especially complex as processes of the operating model are susceptible to contradicting changes. The subsequent part of this paper aims at understanding the impact and the mitigation related to the gap and design requirements for improvement solutions [13].

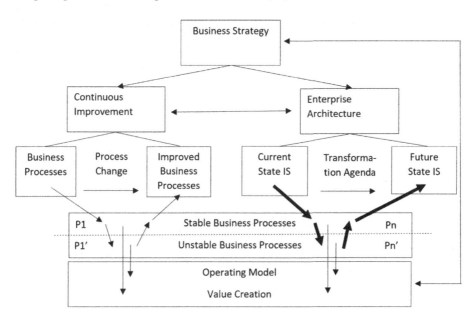

Fig. 1. Mapping of corporate processes

The subsequent part of this paper aims at understanding the impact and the mitigation related to the gap and design requirements for improvement solutions [13]. The theoretical research lens in the case study below is addressing a paradoxical nature suggested in Fig. 1 of business processes and – partly – information systems under change from differing management systems.

4 Case Study

In this section, a case study is presented. The purpose of the case study is to illustrate an organization, where CI and BPM – as two highly important and costly initiatives – have started to diverge and incite suboptimization. The purpose of the case, as including elements of actionable design, is furthermore to consider solutions to the conundrum of concurrent, competing or contradicting management systems as a presumption for productive IS research.

Delight Inc. is a building component producer in the European market with sales units in across Northern Europe and production in Eastern Europe. Delight is formed out of a number of "predecessor" companies merged in an acquisitive process. Administration, manufacturing and IT are cross-organisational where as sales, service and marketing is still connected to the "predecessor" companies as individual brands.

Delight introduced Business Process Management five years ago to prepare for an ERP system implementation (SAP) to consolidate ERP systems of the "predecessor" companies. Processes are defined as standardized processes based both on work practice, best practice and the process conduct stipulated by SAP. The business processes have been documented in the software iGrafx as the documentation has been focused on the to-be stage of the organization in relation to SAP. Delight sees also the business process model as a tool for training, process improvement and cross-national harmonisation.

In order for the organization to react to the changes in the market and as a general principle of lean process governance, Delight introduced alongside BPM a cross-organisational CI program, see Fig. 2. Business units were inspired to grow a culture of CI in line with the philosophy of Lean Manufacturing. The CI program is rooted locally in the organization by e.g. adding CI targets to low level and middle managers contracts, and local level monetary rewards for rapid improvement initiatives. Cross-organisational CI initiatives are rare and assumed difficult due geographic diversity and history of local corporate cultures related to the brands (or "predecessor" companies).

Fig. 2. Delight's setup to identify changes to architecture

The CI program is largely disconnected from the BPM. Some business units and managers have development and implementation of CI initiatives as a KPI. The BPM organization and the SAP implementation effort is challenged due to ongoing CI changes eroding agreed processes and de-harmonising work practices. This is partly contributing to a prolonged SAP implementation process, but is also created from "organizational impatience" with the extended duration of the SAP implementation.

Some initiatives have been started in order to align the CI program with the BPM by creating a project registration tool, were the managers and specialists define the target projects and outline implications.

Architecture is used as an overarching activity to align BPM and IS. Projects must draw on the architectural conceptualizations, while apparent behavior is that CI initiatives overstate emphasis on local processes instead of aligning with architectural considerations. Two examples were identified under the case study that shown the lack of architectural alignment in these projects, with two different problems.

Minicase 1: The purpose of this project was to automate the process of producing AutoCad files from engineering to manufacturing. The project was runned by the Technical Department in X Country, and the solution should be able to draw AutoCad files based on exported data from the as-is ERP system, BaaN. EA was not taken into consideration before beginning the development raising these issues:

- The software was developed to BaaN and not developed to the new ERP system, SAP, that was to be implemented
- The architecture in Delight do not have the data structure to handle the requests from the software, so the data needed is to be extracted and input manually in the software
- The system is developed without no consideration for how to fit into the architecture of the company, not of bad will, but due to lack of insight and "architectural thinking"

A new product configurator was built into the software even though the configurator is built in BaaN. The organization do then have to spend resources for systems maintenance, operations and IT service costs.

Minicase 2: A strategic goal was communicated to the organization to focus on having a better overview of the projects and project status in the subsidiaries. As a response to this call, four different offices in a large subsidiary started development of project management tools. The tools were seen as being at an office level, and no coordination or demand for central solutions were demanded by the subsidiary management. The first project was developed as a manual entry Excel sheet, the second project was developed in SharePoint as a project tool, the third was developed in Excel where the Excel sheet extracted data from systems, and the fourth project was yet another, but different, manual entry Excel sheet. Four different solutions to the same problem with data structured in four different ways. With no architectural overview following problems occurred in this example:

- Four different non-compliant data structures
- Development costs for four project

- Four different data inputs and outputs
- No usages of the standardised business processes across the organization

All projects were implemented in the respectively departments as the architectural standards and policies are non-existing in the CI program, and therefore were both projects accepted in the local organizations (silos).

The case study reveal a close, but not always productive, relationship between the initiatives. Many CI initiatives require IT changes, and IT changes require BPM changes. Characteristically, the initiatives are enacted as small projects with emphasis on short delivery cycles. Furthermore local decision-makers exhibit unawareness of consequences of local level change to the overall benefit of harmonization of processes, "communication in the same language", and reflections to the lack of an adequate services architecture communicated. More than 100 smaller projects were found addressing CI, but not addressing implications for the overall BPM model.

5   Analysis and Solutions

The business processes in Delight need to be aligned with the information technologies in order to make enterprise architecture efforts meaningful in the organization [5]. Delight needs stable and/or controlled business processes in order to reach a successful implementation of SAP [29] and ensure a generally credible governance in respect to e.g. financial reporting and quality assurance. Above is described how EA and CI affects business processes within the gap described in Fig. 1. Subsequently, the development of a methodology for bridging this gap is described.

Business processes were coded with a unique identifier in the set verbal business process documentation. Business processes where then defined through a qualitative elicitation and identification process, and were assigned with a code and a semi-formal definition in the representation tool iGraphx, see Fig. 3. The same code was subsequently used in SAP implementation framework. A tool was created to analyse the alignment of managed business processes in iGraphx and work practices by comparing to transaction codes from SAP. The management analysts can now see, what processes that were executed non-compliant according to the stated definitions, e.g. a salesman issuing a purchase order, or a customer invoice send from a warehouse rather than the account receivables.

Having aligned the systems defined by the EA, and business processes thus enabled measuring of the user behaviour in the organization by matching the permissions from the IT systems, the documented permissions in BPM and the actual IT system usages. With a cross-organisational representation of the IT system and Business Processes, the organization can measure on the level of (mis-) alignment between the elements of business processes, systems and people [34], cf Fig. 4.

Visualizing the technologies and applications that support the activities in the business processes [1] will help the organization to achieve an overview over the EA elements; systems, people and processes [15]. Delight needs to visualize what activities are related to what systems. When this is achieved the focus on getting the holistic overview over the information and data can be identified. Getting the data overview

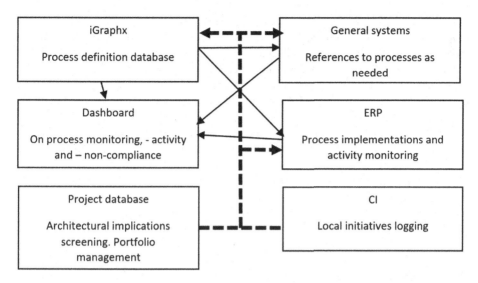

Fig. 3. Diagram of BPM-based process monitoring

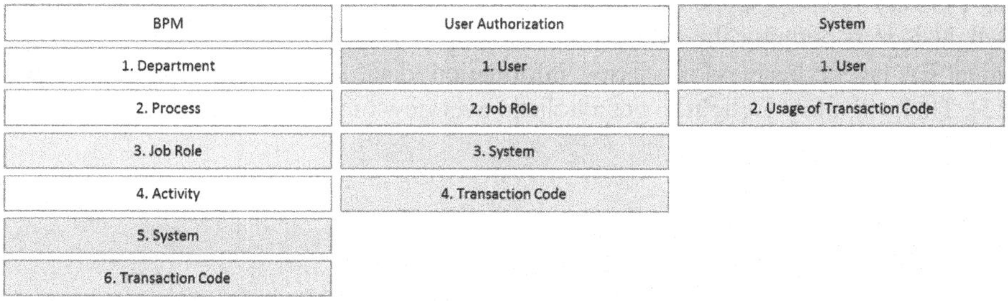

Fig. 4. Overview of how alignment is achieved between System, Business Processes and Authorizations

will then allow Delight to use the data for process performance and then identify process improvements [4].

As identified and presented in the case study Delight is challenged with its CI program running as "silo projects" and without controlled to fit into the architecture, and furthermore not optimized across the different departments. Implementing Enterprise Architecture in Delight will benefit the projects, as the role for EA will then be to identify the changes in the business [13] and to handle the IT development to the overall business strategy [1]. EA will enable identification of cross-project and cross-process capabilities and identify coherence between departments for executive future projects [15].

To include CI in the EA – BPM effort, a process was created, where new projects should be reviewed by an introduced project management office (PMO). The PMO created a form in Microsoft Sharepoint to define the project outline, see Fig. 3. The projects should state if they had implications or requirements for IT or BPM. If they had no implications or requirements for IT or BPM, and budgetary convincing, the project proposal were classified "just do it". If projects had IT or BPM implications, an architectural review was introduced to assess architectural and process implications. If implications were unimportant, projects were likewise passed on to resource allocation. If projects from CI, or any other governance function, had architectural implications, the proposals would go into the EA function like any other request within corporate IT.

EA is setting the guidelines for, how the projects should be develop [14] and define the policies and standards for, how the projects should be designed [14]. Delight defines a long term development plan of EA goals and principles [29] and communicate, how to run an IT project to align with the architecture.

The corporate wide business process coding creates a potential for stopping the gap between EA and CI as a common ontology is established. The organization has an overview of all the transactions a department does, and what permissions each job role needs in the IT system. By aligning BPM and IS an exact overview of the business job roles is defined, and what activities roles have permissions to perform, and what they actually do perform [34]. In addition Integrating IS and BPM will increase Delight's ability to integrate and align IT, processes and people in the EA [34].

Delight has only documented the business processes for the future state. Absence of current state processes is unfortunate in lengthy implementation projects. Customers can't clearly identify scope and focal transformation requirements. The next step for Delight is start defining the ever-present current state of the EA by defining the individual EA layers; business processes, information, data, applications and technologies [15]. This will allow Delight to get a holistic overview of the current architecture in the organization [1].

6   Discussion

BPM and CI are both highly ranked on the agendas of transformation in companies [6–8]. In this discussion these concepts are highlighted against EA to add to our understanding of EA as mean for balancing short-term and long-term transformation. In a tradition of information systems studies the concepts of BPM and CI must be brought to work in synergy in order to overcome barriers for transformation and implementation. The presented conflicting positions between BPM and CI must be switched into mutual support and avoid a zero-sum game process. In the BPM-CI intersection we see EA as an explanatory frame of reference. EA embody strategy and the translation of business strategy into the operating model and technology.

In Fig. 1, the interrelation between EA, CI and BPM is stated, but realizing that in scenarios like Delight, contradictions to "single line" of corporate governance is giving problems. The business processes are dynamic and the dynamics originate from different parallel governance regimes. BPM can't be established as only being "owned" by the EA practice. CI practice is just as well affected business processes. The thin lines out of CI in Fig. 1 indicate rapid changes on local levels, whereas the bold lines from EA indicate a less agile and a more resource consuming transformation agenda. EA coordinates technology in relation to strategy. CI do not necessarily have any responsibility to the technological dimension of the organization. Traditionally, business processes are embodied in the EA stack. The study pinpoint other stakeholders than EA. Ironically this calls for a framework for governance of frameworks for corporate governance.

Figure 1 underscore that the operating model of the company will need to navigate in both stable and unstable business processes. The risk of counterproductivity increase as changes are anchored in uncoordinated organizational entities pursuing governance opportunistically e.g. fueled by individual contracts and performance measures. Synchronisation between change becomes critical.

A key theoretical contribution of this paper is the necessity to understand organization dynamics at a process level from the influencing governance regimes. A theoretical contribution is furthermore that there will probably be a significant level of unstable processes imposing challenges to precision in any BPM-founded IS requirements specification. Having centralized process monitoring technologies is significantly helping EA processes following the fundamentals of Ross [14] but observing dynamics in unified as well as diversified operating models. The described implementation of identification, monitoring and screening models suggests that more stable and controllable environments can be realized over time.

The architectural knowledge needs to be achieved through a holistic overview of the current state of the technologies, databases, applications and processes across the organization [14, 15] potentially contradicting local innovativeness. Architectural policies and standards for how to design technologies, databases and application need to be defined [14] and to create a team to develop and maintain IT to deliver solutions to the organization in order to support the changing business objectives [1].

Learning outcomes of the case is that without an organizational architectural awareness and without architectural control, the CI program will run as individual projects at a decentralised level, where the departmental processes are optimized and not the process across departments. This is in line with the theory of Feral Information Systems [27] that are developed to satisfy user needs without alignment with other systems or overall process flow in the organization.

The case and discussion highlight the issue of concurrent or competent corporate governance frameworks in this case CI and EA. It contradicts EA as a top level strategic framework, but is more leading to an understanding of EA one out more, and an importance in EA to include non-EA initiatives into the management plan or transformation agenda. Likewise stable business processes are a problematic perception of working practices. In this sense, CI contradicts BPM by constantly seek change whereas EA-driven BPM seeks stability. Gartners outline of the bimodal (or two-speed) IT organization might solve the matter [35] but doesn't address the risk of losing BPM's bid for harmonized processes. Solutions lie in coordination, synchronization, training, mutual awareness of central and decentral change processes, and a more and more embracing EA.

7 Conclusions

This paper has focused on EA, BPM and CI and the complex and partly contradictory relationship between these elements. A qualitative case study has identified several elements in this area for achieving alignment of the EA with business processes, and how EA can question the challenges in organizations with CI programs.

This paper has demonstrated that running CI programs without an overall control of the Enterprise Architecture will end up with extra costs, silo projects and non-integrated solutions. A gap between EA and CI has been derived from the literature review. The gap is affected process stability in the operating model. Conflicting governance regimes are detrimental to corporate performance at the level of business process and operating model. The paper is describing how the case company developed tools for company wide business process coding and identification connected to the systems of SAP and iGraphx together with supporting systems ("dashboard") for following up on non-compliance. Additionally a project governance model were introduced with any project proposal being screened for architectural implications.

Organizations need to support the CI projects with technical knowledge and implement EA policies and standards in order to control projects not be become silo projects. Integrating a process focus in the improvement projects can identify, what processes that will change in the future stage and create an overview of what systems need changing. By adding this the CI program will then add value to the Enterprise Architectural overview.

As suggestions for further work it will be interesting to investigate, what the effect of implementing information and data into the business model will reflect in the holistic overview for the architecture. If the organizations know what data is generated where and how the data flow is through the business processes will allow the organization to achieve higher data quality and ensure cross sharing of information. It will also be interesting to identify if information and data implementation can add controllability to the CI program and be part of identifying processes to improve by running simulations based on the data.

References

1. Khayami, R.: Qualitative characteristics of enterprise architecture. Procedia Comput. Sci. **3**, 1277–1282 (2011)
2. Bernus, P.: Enterprise models for enterprise architecture and ISO9000:2000. Annu. Rev. Control **27**, 211–220 (2003)
3. Holm, H., Buschle, M., Ekstedt, M., Lagerström, R.: Automatic data collection for enterprise architecture models. Softw. Syst. Model. **13**, 825–841 (2014)
4. Jensen, C.T.: Integrating EA and BPM synergisticaly. In: IEEE Conference on Commerce and Enterprise Computing, pp. 279–285 (2011)
5. Lankhorst, M.M.: Enterprise architecture modelling - the issue of integration. Adv. Eng. Inform. **18**, 205–2016 (2005)
6. Eaidgah, Y., et al.: Visual management, performance management and continuous improvement: a lean manufacturing approach. Int. J. Lean Six Sigma **7**(2), 187–210 (2016)

7. Singh, J., Singh, H.: Continuous improvement philosophy–literature review and directions. Benchmarking Int. J. **22**(1), 75–119 (2015)
8. Yang, Y., Lee, P., Cheng, T.: Continuous improvement competence, employee creativity, and new service development performance: a frontline employee perspective. Int. J. Prod. Econ. **171**, 275–288 (2016)
9. Kitchenham, B., Charters, S.: Guidelines for performing Systematic Literature Reviews in Software Engineering. Software Engineering Group (2007)
10. Saunders, M., Lewis, P., Thornhill, A.: Research Methods for Business Students, 5th edn. Pearson Education, London. (2009)
11. Walsham, G.: Doing interpretive research. Eur. J. Inf. Syst. **15**(3), 320–330 (2006)
12. Goldkuhl, G.: Pragmatism vs interpretivism in qualitative information systems research. Eur. J. Inf. Syst. **21**(2), 135–146 (2012)
13. Peffers, K., Tuunanen, T., Rothenberger, M.A., Chatterjee, S.: A design science research methodology for information systems research. J. Manag. Inf. Syst. **24**(3), 45–77 (2007)
14. Ross, J.W.: Creating a Strategic IT Architecture Competency: Learning in Stages. MIT CISR (2003)
15. Cram, A., Brohman, K., Gallupe, B.: Addressing the control challenges of the enterprise architecture process. J. Inf. Syst. **29**(2), 161–182 (2015)
16. Rajabi, Z., Abade, M.N.: Data-centric enterprise architecture. Inf. Eng. Electron. Bus. **4**(4), 53–60 (2012)
17. Shuja, A.K.: Enterprise Architecture: What is it and why should we care? (2016). http://www.shuja.info/publications.html
18. Pontacoloni, M.: SearchSOA (2010). http://searchsoa.techtarget.com/tip/Enterprise-architects-can-use-BPMN-as-common-language-for-process-modeling. Accessed 18 Nov 2016
19. van Steenbergen, M., van den Berg, M., Brinkkemper, S.: A balanced approach to developing the enterprise architecture practice. In: Filipe, J., Cordeiro, J., Cardoso, J. (eds.) ICEIS 2007. LNBIP, vol. 12, pp. 240–253. Springer, Heidelberg (2008). https://doi.org/10.1007/978-3-540-88710-2_19
20. Dietz, J.L., Hoogervorst, J.A., Albani, A., Aveiro, D., Babkin, E., Barjis, J., Caetano, A., Huysmans, P., Iijima, J., van Kervel, S., Mulder, H.: The discipline of enterprise engineering. Int. J. Organ. Des. Eng. **3**(1), 86–114 (2013)
21. Hope, T., Chew, E., Sharma, R.: The failure of success factors: lessons from success and failure cases of enterprise architecture implementation. In: Proceedings of the 2017 ACM SIGMIS Conference on Computers and People Research, pp. 21–27. ACM (2017)
22. Seppänen, V.: From problems to critical success factors of enterprise architecture adoption. Ph.D. dissertation, Jyväskylä Studies in Computing, p. 201 (2014)
23. Hines, P., Taylor, D., Walsh, A.: The Lean journey: have we got it wrong? Total Qual. Manag. Bus. Excell. 1–18 (2018)
24. McCann, L., Hassard, J.S., Granter, E., Hyde, P.J.: Casting the lean spell: the promotion, dilution and erosion of lean management in the NHS. Hum. Relat. **68**(10), 1557–1577 (2015)
25. Näslund, D.: Lean, six sigma and lean sigma: fads or real process improvement methods? Bus. Process Manag. J. **14**(3), 269–287 (2008)
26. Trkman, P.: Increasing process orientation with business process management: critical practices'. Int. J. Inf. Manag. **33**(1), 48–60 (2013)
27. Bækgaard, L., Olsen, M., Tambo, T.: Architectural issues related to feral information systems. In: Feral Information Systems Development: Managerial Implications. Business Science Reference, pp. 227–241 (2014)

28. Rouhani, B.D.: A systematic literature review on Enterprise Architecture Implementation Methodologies. Inf. Softw. Technol. **62**, 1–20 (2015)
29. von Rosing, M., Hove, M., Subbarao, R. Preston, T.W.: Combining BPM and EA in complex IT projects, pp. 271–278. Computer Society (2011)
30. Witts, I.: Triaster (2016). http://blog.triaster.co.uk/blog/bpm-vs-ea-pros-cons-benefits-drawbacks
31. Kemsley, S.: Column2 (2011). http://www.slideshare.net/skemsley/aligning-bpm-and-ea
32. Schooff, P.: ebiz (2012). http://www.ebizq.net/blogs/ebizq_forum/2012/09/what-role-does-bpm-play-in-enterprise-architecture.php
33. Barros, A., Dumas, M., ter Hofstede, A.H.M.: Service interaction patterns. In: van der Aalst, Wil M.P., Benatallah, B., Casati, F., Curbera, F. (eds.) BPM 2005. LNCS, vol. 3649, pp. 302–318. Springer, Heidelberg (2005). https://doi.org/10.1007/11538394_20
34. Clausen, N.: ERP and BPM - a report tool for measuring level of alignment. Aarhus University (2015)
35. Gartner Inc.: Bimodal (2014). http://www.gartner.com/it-glossary/bimodal/

Mobile Applications as Carriers of Institutional Pressures: A Case of the Finnish Taxi Industry

Karin Väyrynen[1(✉)], Arto Lanamäki[1], and Juho Lindman[2]

[1] Interact Research Unit, Faculty of ITEE, University of Oulu,
PO Box 8000, 90014 Oulun Yliopisto, Finland
{karin.vayrynen, arto.lanamaki}@oulu.fi
[2] Applied Information Technology,
University of Gothenburg, Gothenburg, Sweden
juho.lindman@ait.gu.se

Abstract. While the worldwide market expansion of Uber has raised controversy, Uber has also received praise for its mobile phone app. Its many features – taxi ordering, pricing, real-time location information, paying, and service evaluation – have provided significant customer value. When Uber entered Finland in November 2014, few other taxi apps were available. Between 2014 and 2018, this shortage of taxi apps turned into an abundance, with many companies introducing their own taxi apps. By leaning on institutional theory, and more specifically by applying coercive, mimetic and normative pressures as a lens, we provide an explanation for why three Finnish taxi apps now resemble Uber in some features, whereas they differ in others. Based on our interviews, we can explain the present-day differences between these apps by coercive and normative pressures in the institutional environment of the Finnish taxi industry. We contribute to the IT and institutionalization research stream by illustrating how mobile applications as IT artefacts can be seen as carriers of institutional pressures materializing in the features they provide.

Keywords: Taxi industry · Institutional pressures · Mobile apps

1 Introduction

The fame of the transportation network company Uber is mostly associated with its affordable "ridesharing" service UberX (known as UberPop in some markets) [1]. Uber's worldwide expansion has fueled controversy [2] and the company's ethics have been questioned [3, 4]. Yet, Uber's mobile app is generally viewed as an impressive technological achievement [5]. Largely due to Uber, the taxi industry is now one of the most well-known examples of industry-transforming digital disruption [2, 5].

Theories of organizational institutionalism have discussed change and stability when evaluating the impacts of digital technologies in various industries. Earlier research has treated these technologies as exogenous change forces, but a more nuanced understanding of their endogenous role has recently emerged [6].

Studies on institutional theory have shown that firms face multiple institutional pressures that are often incompatible with each other [7]. Gosain [8] argues that

© Springer International Publishing AG, part of Springer Nature 2018
S. D. Müller and J. A. Nielsen (Eds.): SCIS 2018, LNBIP 326, pp. 55–68, 2018.
https://doi.org/10.1007/978-3-319-96367-9_5

institutional logics are encoded into IT systems. Rajão and Hayes ([9], p. 328) formulate that "institutional theory can provide an important theoretical lens to provide a historical understanding of the ways in which specific IT artefacts come about and change over time". They look at the institutional context in form of conceptualizations of control and argue that there is a dialectic relationship between the institutional context and the IT artefact. IT artefacts are "bundles of material and cultural properties packaged in some socially recognizable form such as hardware and/or software" ([10], p. 121). Along these lines, mobile taxi hailing applications represent such IT artefacts.

The institutional environment of Finnish taxi firms has been heavily regulated. Finland has one of the tightest barriers to entry in the taxi market in the EU [11]. The number of taxi licenses is limited and the maximum price for taxi rides is regulated by the state. Taxi drivers have to pass a test and are required to use the official taximeter in their cars. Thus, the institutional environment for taxi hailing organizations and their IT artifacts in form of mobile apps is especially interesting in Finland. In November 2014, Uber entered the Finnish taxi market. Between November 2014 and the present day (February 2018), several mobile taxi hailing applications have been introduced in Finland by existing Finnish taxi companies.

Leaning on Rajão and Hayes [9], we wondered how the institutional context in a form of different institutional pressures in Finland can help explain the similarities, but also the differences between three Finnish taxi hailing apps and Uber. We ask the following research question:

> How are institutional pressures implicated in the feature functionalities in taxi hailing apps in the Finnish market?

Our main contribution is to show that applying the lens of institutional pressures can help explain why mobile apps that were created for similar purposes resemble each other in some features, while they differ in other features. We illustrate how IT artefacts in form of mobile apps can be seen as carriers of institutional pressures.

2   Theoretical Background

We ground our study in literature on institutional theory, and more specifically, on institutional pressures, and the inscription of institutional values into IT artefacts.

Institutional theory helps explain why organizations within a certain institutional environment resemble each other. Institutions mean regulative, normative, and cognitive structures and activities that provide stability and meaning to social behavior [12]. Organizations operate in institutional environments, and in order to receive legitimacy and support they have to conform to the rules and requirements of these environments. Institutional isomorphism means that firms subscribe to the same institutions within their field [13], and that organizations/units resemble other units in that same environment. Three forms of institutional pressures/forces that lead to institutional isomorphism can be distinguished: coercive, normative, and mimetic [13].

Coercive pressures are results of politics and power relationships in the society. Actors such as the state require compliance in practices threatening with formal and informal sanctions. In coercive isomorphism, companies of an industry show similarities to each other because of certain regulative or legal pressures. *Normative pressures* are results of what is considered proper course of action and often related to professional values. In normative isomorphism, change is influenced by professional standards or networks. *Mimetic pressures* are a reaction to uncertainty: organizations follow examples that are evaluated as being successful. In mimetic isomorphism, thus, a company imitates another company because of assuming that the other company's structure is somehow beneficial. Regulative pressures often come top-down from governments, whereas mimetic pressures are result of peer-pressure from other companies and normative pressures come from professional groups primarily from inside organizations [14].

IS research has also applied institutional theory extensively. Mignerat and Rivard [15] analyzed 53 IS studies that use institutional theory. They identified entities from which institutional pressures arise from in four stages of IS innovation. They found that coercive pressures arise from, e.g., governments, regulatory agencies and industry associations, normative pressures from, e.g., technology suppliers, industry and trade associations and consultants, and mimetic pressures from, e.g., peers, successful organizations, and competition.

Researchers have brought IT artefacts into the study of institutional theory. Rajão and Hayes [9] identified four research streams regarding the relationship between organizations and IT artifacts: (1) why organizations still invest into IT even though no clear evidence exists about increased efficiency and return-on-investment, (2) IT innovations, (3) the inscription of institutional values into IT artefacts, and (4) the role of IT artefacts in change processes. Our research falls into the third category. Rajão and Hayes ([9], p. 321), building on [16], summarize that "the context of institutions find their way into the design of IT artefacts, which in turn also become institutional carriers that help to support and reproduce certain institutional arrangements".

In the present paper, we study how institutional pressures are implicated in the features of three Finnish taxi-hailing apps.

3   Research Methods and Context

3.1   Research Methods

We conducted this research as a case study, which is a suitable approach in addressing "how" and "why" questions about a contemporary phenomenon [17]. As the current research asks how institutional pressures are implicated in different features of taxi hailing apps available in the Finnish market, case study is a suitable research method.

Case Background. This paper is part of a research program investigating digitalization in the Finnish taxi service industry. In the present study, we compare the features implemented in three Finnish taxi apps to the traditional taxi service model on the one hand, and the Uber app on the other hand. We selected these three apps as they are by far the "largest" ones in Finland when looking at the number of taxis that can be reached with the applications. *App A* (7500 taxis in 200 municipalities in Finland) has been launched in 2015 and works nationwide. *App B* (1250 taxis in Southern Finland) was launched in June 2015 by a taxi dispatch center that dispatches rides in 19 cities in

Southern Finland. *App C* (1335 taxis in Southern Finland) has been launched by Southern Taxi (a pseudonym) in November 2017. Before that, Southern Taxi had already another mobile app (Delta App) with much more restricted feature functionalities than App C. Southern Taxi used App A in parallel to the Delta App for almost 2 years but separated from App A in November 2017.

Data Collection. We collected publicly available information on the features of App A, B and C and Uber from the respective websites of the applications. We have read histories of the taxi service industry in Finland (e.g., [18]) and elsewhere (e.g., [19]). Moreover, we have followed public discussion on the media concerning the taxi service industry. In addition, we conducted 17 interviews with 18 interviewees (one interview was a group interview with 2 interviewees) with an average length of 88.4 min (see Table 1). Interviewees were representatives of the taxi companies of App A and App C, technology providers of App A and App C, representatives of Uber Finland, as well as dispatch centers who use(d) App A. In addition, we interviewed representatives of other taxi companies and taxi industry stakeholders in Finland. For anonymization reasons, we are not able to give more detailed information about which interviewee represented which company. Our comparison of the features of App A, B, C and Uber is mainly based on publicly available information. Our understanding of the institutional environment in which App A-C were developed is based on the interviews.

Table 1. List of interviewees (anonymized).

#	Title	Organization
1	Executive manager	FTOF
2	Executive manager	FTOF
3	Manager	FTOF
4	Executive manager	Technology provider for FTOF
5	Manager	Southern Taxi
6	Executive manager/Developer	Technology provider for Southern Taxi
7	Executive manager	Northern Taxi
8	Executive manager	Northern Taxi
9	Representative	Uber Finland
10	Lobbyist	A PR Agency
11	Representative	Taxify
12	Executive manager	A regional taxi service association
13	Executive manager	A regional taxi service company
14	Executive manager	Transportation service company
15	Executive manager	A technology provider
16	Chief of licensing	A public sector organization
17	Entrepreneur	A technology provider
18	Expert	A mobility association

Data Analysis. In the data analysis, we made use of the five aspects of the basic process related to ride sourcing platforms [5] that are relevant to the customer. These five aspects are (1) requesting a ride in real time via a smart-phone application, (2) viewing the vehicle's real-time location and estimated arrival time while waiting, (3) automatic payment of the ride through the credit card registered with the app, – (4) where pricing can respond dynamically to demand – and (5) rider and driver rating each other after completion of the ride. In the first step of the analysis, we analyzed how these aspects were implemented in the features of the apps. In the second step, we compared these to the traditional Finnish taxi ride sourcing process and found that the Finnish taxi apps resemble in some aspects the traditional taxi hailing process in Finland, and in some aspects Uber. In the third step, we used the concepts of coercive, normative and mimetic pressures [13] as an analytical lens to help explain the similarities and differences between these features in the three Finnish apps and the Uber app concerning these five aspects. We focus our analysis on the time span from Uber's entry in the Finnish market in November 2014 to the present day situation (February 2018). We analyze how the institutional environment shaped these three Finnish mobile apps.

3.2   Institutional Context: The Finnish Taxi Service Industry

The idea of taxi services is virtually uniform everywhere: driving a car for a fee to get a customer from point A to point B. However, the Finnish taxi industry differs from the taxi industry in many other countries. Taxi driver-owners are highly unionized as more than 80% of Finnish taxi drivers belong to the FTOF. Due to the legal framework and high level of unionization, the taxi service industry has provided a rather uniform service everywhere in Finland, costing about the same price at all times. The Finnish government sets the maximum prices for taxis yearly. Finnish taxis are perceived as safe and reliable, even though perhaps costly. All taxi cars have a taximeter and taxi drivers pay taxes loyally. Customers receive receipts for their taxi trips, and the taximeter provides data on all trips. The Finnish taxation office has legal rights to access the taximeter data by request. Due to the aforementioned factors, gray economy has not been a significant factor in the Finnish taxi sector.

Uber entered the Finnish market in November 2014. In August 2017, Uber exited the Finnish market because of being ruled as not conforming to the law in Finland. Uber has announced its return to the Finnish market in July 2018, when the new deregulative Act on Transport Services is enacted in Finland.[1]

---

[1] https://www.lvm.fi/act-on-transport-services (15.5.2018)

4   Findings

In the time between November 2014 and February 2018, a number of taxi hailing apps have been introduced in the Finnish market. In this analysis, we focus on the three major – when counting the number of taxis that can be reached with the app – Finnish mobile applications for taxi hailing: App A, App B and App C *(pseudonyms)*.

App B and App C are used by only one dispatch center each. App A, in contrast, has been integrated with 30 Finnish taxi dispatch centers. These centers use five different types of dispatch technologies, and as App A should look and feel the same way to customers all over Finland the different technical requirements set certain limits to the functionalities that have been implemented in App A so far.

When we refer to all of these Finnish taxi apps collectively, we refer to them as "Taxi apps", otherwise we refer to them as App A, B and C. Next, we will describe how ride requesting, real-time location, paying, pricing and rating in these Taxi apps differ from or are similar to the Uber app features, and how institutional pressures help explain the resemblance or difference. Figure 1 summarizes our findings.

4.1   Requesting a Ride

Starting from the 1950s, customers have been able to call a taxi dispatch center to order a taxi in Finland. Since the beginning of the 21st century, it was also possible to order a taxi via a text message.

With all Finnish Taxi apps, the passenger uses the mobile application to order a ride. The reason that this additional channel for ordering a car was provided to the customers was related to progressing digitalization and customer expectations in general:

> "*Everyone knew about [the new entrants]. Uber came to Helsinki in the end of 2014. Taxify was another one that entered in 2014, in Oulu. Those brought the message that people wanted to use [hailing apps]. And if one thinks about our operation model, that you have to call and don't even always know where to call, [having an app] was self-evident...*" (Interviewee #3)."

Mimetic Pressure: As digital taxi hailing channels were successful and customers were using them when such channels were available, also the Finnish taxi organizations wanted to provide this to customers.

4.2   Real-Time Location

Already since 2003, the dispatch centers have had location information of the taxis. While the taxi drivers have used GPS navigation for the last two decades, customers did not have access to this information.

All Taxi apps as well as Uber allow for automatic determination of the customer's location. This automatic location determination is used as the assumed address the customer wants to get the taxi to. Once a driver has accepted the requested ride, the estimated arrival time of the taxi is being displayed in all of the Taxi apps as well as the

Uber app. The Uber app, App B and App C show the approaching taxi on a map to the customer. App A provides this service only for the Helsinki area, not for other geographic areas in Finland.

Important here is that all app providers see the value of providing real-time location information through the app. Lack of provision is mainly due to difficulties, costs, or coordination challenges related to integration between different dispatch systems:

> *"A technical challenge is that ... how to provide the user a good and consistent user experience everywhere. Now, when you order a taxi with [App A] in Oulu, you don't see the location information, you only get the arrival estimate. But when you order in Helsinki, you see the car in real time on your screen. This is because the different dispatch centers and other systems have different capabilities. We don't get the same data from different systems. All this scattered data has to be provided consistently to the user."* (Interviewee #3)

Mimetic Pressure: Having real-time information about the taxi's location on a map visible for the customer is one of the core features of Uber and other ride hailing apps (e.g., Estonia-based Taxify and US-based Lyft). App B and App C provide this feature, and App A provides it for Helsinki. For App A, this feature is also envisioned to be implemented for the rest of Finland, but *technical challenges* related to having to integrate several different types of dispatch centers with App A slowed down the implementation of this feature.

4.3   Paying

Since the beginning of taxi history in Finland, payment for the ride has been provided directly to the driver at the end of the ride. Card payment has been possible in Finnish taxis since 1980s.

Uber offers *only* automatic credit card payment through the application. It does not allow a cash payment. In contrast, customers using a Taxi app always have the option to pay for the ride in cash or by credit card directly to the driver in the taxi. Automatic credit card payment is not available in App A and B. Also the dispatch centers using App A would have liked to have this feature in App A. However, due to the *technical restrictions* stemming from some of the types of dispatch technology used in Finland, this feature has not yet been implemented. App C, in contrast, allows the customer to pay automatically through the app by credit card. Uber was seen as a "role model" with this feature:

> *Uber showed one thing. They were the first app where you did not have to pay separately. [...] Uber users were praising this. Of course, there were other apps around the world [with app-based payments]. Uber did not invent it, but it succeeded to break through. [...] It started this hype."* (Interviewee #5)

The possibility to implement this feature was one of the reasons why Southern Taxi decided to use their own app instead of App A. They wanted to have full control over the development of features in a situation of rising competition starting from July 2018.

Table 2. Comparison of traditional taxi industry, App A, App B, App C and Uber across the five aspects of the taxi hailing process

	Requesting	Viewing real-time location on a map	Automatic credit card payment	Surge pricing	Rating
Traditional taxi industry	Phone call, text message, hailing taxi down on street	No information about real-time location of ordered taxi available to customer.	Not available. Payment usually to the driver either in cash or via credit card in the taxi.	No. Maximum price for taxi rides based on measurement of time and/or distance is yearly set by Finnish government.	Feedback given to driver directly or to "taxi inspectors" who help solve conflicts between customer and driver.
App A	Mobile app	Available only in Helsinki. In the rest of Finland, the app displayed the estimated time of taxi arrival only.	Not available. Payment to the driver either in cash or via credit card in the taxi.	No. Pricing pre-defined in adherence to pricing rules set by Finnish government.	Customers can rate drivers. Drivers cannot rate customers.
App B	Mobile app	Available	Not available. Payment to the driver either in cash or via credit card in the taxi.	No. Pricing pre-defined in adherence to pricing rules set by Finnish government.	Customers can rate drivers. Drivers cannot rate customers.
App C	Mobile app	Available	Available	No. Pricing pre-defined in adherence to pricing rules set by Finnish government.	Customers can rate drivers. Drivers cannot rate customers.
Uber	Mobile app	Available	Available	Surge pricing in use.	Customers can rate drivers, and drivers can rate customers.
Institutional pressure type	Mimetic	Coercive	Mimetic	Mimetic	Mimetic; normative

Mimetic Pressure: App C was launched in preparation for the fierce competition that is being expected to arise especially in the Helsinki area after the de-regulation of the taxi industry through the new Act on Transport Services. Southern Taxi decided to give up using App A in order to be able to fully make use of the technical abilities and data provided by the dispatch software used in its own dispatch center. Having the opportunity to automatically pay via credit card is one of the core features of Uber and other ride hailing apps (e.g., Estonia-based Taxify and US-based Lyft). Thus, concerning App C, the implementation of this feature can be seen to result from mimetic pressure. In addition, this feature is also wished for and intended for implementation in future in App A, but just as is the case with real-time location information, the technical challenges stemming from having to integrate several different taxi dispatch technologies with App A slowed down the implementation of this feature in App A.

4.4   Pricing

Throughout the history of Finnish taxi, the government of Finland has regulated taxi pricing. Maximum prices for traditional taxi rides are decided upon yearly by the Finnish government. For example, it is defined that taxi companies can bill a fee of around 7 euros if a customer pre-orders a taxi more than 30 min before the ride. Currently, all taxis in Finland have to have a measurement device – a taximeter – that calculates the price based on the regulation set by the government. Prices for taxi rides ordered with a Finnish Taxi app always correspond to the prices set by the government.

Pricing in Uber, on the other hand, can respond dynamically to demand for and supply of rides. When demand exceeds supply, the service switches to surge pricing mode, where rides can be very costly.

Coercive Pressure: As taxi ride pricing is regulated by the Finnish government, none of the Finnish Taxi apps incorporates surge pricing, which is an essential part of Uber's business model and the Uber app. The coercive pressure exercised by the government helps explain on the one hand why pricing is implemented in the same way in all Finnish apps, and on the other hand why Finnish apps do *not* resemble Uber in regard to pricing.

4.5   Rating

Ever since unionization started occurring in 1950s [18], there has been an expectation that Finnish taxi services provide a standardized level of service. This has meant that taxi drivers follow the occupational code of quality service, and by consequence, there is no need to establish a rating system. While customers regularly give feedback about the service, rating has not been part of the profession.

All Taxi apps allow the customer to rate the taxi driver, but not the other way round. Uber, on the other hand, enables a two-way evaluation: drivers evaluate customers, and customers evaluate drivers.

In App A it seems that this driver-customer rating is deliberately left out, as the answer to the question "Does the taxi driver give feedback about the customer?" in the FAQ section on the website of App A states:

> "In [App A], drivers do not evaluate customers. The Finnish taxi serves all of its customers with equally high quality".

In addition, several interviewees pointed to the requirement of taxi drivers to be very socially skilled to be able to offer high-quality service to all kinds of customers, also in difficult situations (e.g., picking up someone from the hospital who was just diagnosed with cancer). The general tenor is that taxi drivers are professionals who are skilled in dealing with different types of customers:

> "I don't see it important to rate customers. (…) In the end, we need to respect every customer. We need to be humble. I do understand the Uber rating system, that if a customer is difficult, then the customer pays a price for that. But we will not do that. We need to have enough workmanship and flexibility to serve all kinds of customers." (Interviewee #7)

Regarding the rating features, both mimetic and normative pressure help explain similarities and differences between Finnish Taxi apps and Uber.

Mimetic Pressure: The possibility of customers rating service providers and the other way around has become a common feature in apps and the sharing economy. Taxify, Uber and AirBnB make use of this feature, and in the case of customers being able to rate drivers, it seems that mimetic pressure is at play.

Normative Pressure: Where Uber enforces that drivers rate their customer, this feature is (deliberately) left out from Finnish Taxi apps. It seems that the decision to exclude the driver-customer rating is a result of certain standards the taxi associations have set for the taxi driver occupation and represents an example of how normative pressure affects taxi app features.

4.6   Summary

Figure 1 summarizes our findings. We show for each feature whether Finnish Taxi apps resemble the traditional Finnish taxi hailing process (i.e., the grey bar crosses the line between "Traditional" and "Finnish Taxi apps") or Uber (i.e., the grey bar crosses the line between "Finnish Taxi apps" and "Uber"). For two features – real-time location information and paying – some apps resemble the traditional taxi hailing process, whereas other apps resemble Uber. Even though for App A the wish exists to provide real-time location information and automatic credit card payment, mostly technical challenges and limitations are reasons for why the app differs from Uber. Rating is separated into whether customers can rate drivers (Customer –> Driver) and whether drivers can rate customers (Driver -> Customer).

	Traditional	Finnish Taxi apps	Uber	Forms of institutional pressures
Requesting		App A, B, C		**Mimetic pressure**: Mobile apps have become normal and expected in most types of industries. They are a legitimate distribution channel for ordering services also in the taxi industry.
Pricing	App A, B, C			**Coercive pressure**. None of the Finnish taxi apps, e.g., has surge pricing as Uber does, due to price regulations by the Finnish government
Real-time location information	App A	App A, B, C		**Mimetic pressure**: Real-time location information is available in all Finnish taxi apps at least for the Helsinki area. App A does not provide this feature for other areas than Helsinki yet, but this is due to the technical challenges of integrating different types of taxi ride distribution centers, not because of coercive or normative pressures.
Paying	App A, B	App C		**Mimetic pressure**. Uber's cash-less payment feature has been seen to be beneficial. App C has implemented this feature, App A intends to implement it in future.
Rating Customer -> Driver		App A, B, C		**Mimetic pressure**: all Finnish taxi apps, as well as Uber, allow rating the ride/driver. Customer ratings have been widely adopted also in other sharing economy platforms, e.g., AirBnB.
Driver -> Customer	App A, B, C			**Normative pressure**: none of the Finnish taxi apps allows the driver to rate the customer as Uber does. One reason are the norms associated with the taxi profession in Finland, where taxi drivers serve all customers (also difficult ones) without judging the customer.

Fig. 1. Coercive, normative, and mimetic pressures in the features of Finnish taxi hailing apps

5 Discussion

We set out to answer how institutional pressures are implicated in the feature functionalities of Finnish taxi hailing apps. With our analysis in the previous section, we demonstrated how different types of institutional pressures help explain similarities and differences between the Finnish mobile apps on the one hand, and features of the mobile app provided by the disruptive model of Uber (cf. [20, 21]) on the other hand. Our main contribution lies in illustrating how mobile applications as IT artefacts are carriers of institutional pressures that materialize in the features of the IT artifact.

Previous research has already addressed the encodement of institutional logics into IT systems [4] and argued for applying institutional theory as a historical understanding of how certain IT artefacts come about over time [9]. With this study, we contribute to research on institutionalization and IT by illustrating how features of mobile applications are affected by three types of institutional pressures: mimetic, coercive and normative. The Uber app has been praised by customers and competitors alike. We found that mimetic pressures are reflected in certain features of Finnish mobile apps (e.g., real-time location information and payment), most clearly in App C which prepares for the increased competition that is expected to arise after the de-regulation of the Finnish taxi industry in July 2018. We found that the Finnish government's coercive pressure in form of taxi price regulation is reflected in the pricing feature of Finnish Taxi apps. Coercive pressures apply to all organizations in a specific field [13] – in this case the Finnish taxi industry. This helps explain why all Finnish apps differ from Uber regarding pricing. We also found that normative pressures in form of certain standards regarding the taxi driver profession and upheld by the FTOF and taxi organizations are reflected in not allowing drivers to rate their customers in Finnish

Taxi apps. Our findings are supported by Mignerat and Rivard [15]. They found that in IT innovation processes, coercive pressures are exercised, amongst others, by governments, and mimetic pressures, for example, by competitors (which Uber can be seen to represent).

We also contribute to research on the relationship between institutional environment and IT artefacts by taking a somewhat different approach than extant research. Much of previous research on institutional theory and IS focused on the effects of the institutional environment on IT adoption and use [22–24], or the institutional effects in IT innovation and interaction between IT and institutions [15]. We, in contrast, focused on the effect of institutional pressures on mobile app features. Just as Rajão and Hayes [9] found that the design of IT artefacts tends to reflect the currently dominant conceptions of control, we found that the design of mobile apps (which are IT artefacts) reflects different institutional pressures.

Specifically in the Finnish taxi industry, there is a long history of the profession of taxi drivers, and taxi services are generally of a high standard. The Finnish taxi industry thus differs greatly from, e.g., the North American taxi services, which have been described as substandard [5].

With our research, we applied principles of the institutional theory from the organizational level to the mobile app feature level. Institutional theory has been applied to explain why organizations start to resemble each other [13]. We showed that the concept of institutional pressures can explain both similarities and differences between features of IT artifacts. Similarly to how institutions are "carriers of histories" [25], IT artifacts such as mobile applications are carriers of institutional pressures.

6 Conclusion

In this paper, we applied the three types of institutional pressures (normative, mimetic, coercive) as an analytical lens to help explain why three Finnish taxi hailing apps on the one hand resembled – and on the other hand differ from – the Uber app. We focused on five app features: (1) ride requesting, (2) pricing, (3) providing real-time location information, (4) paying, and (5) rating.

We found that (1) coercive pressures exercised from the Finnish government help explain why pricing in all three Finnish apps resembles each other whereas it differs from Uber, (2) normative pressures explain why none of the Finnish apps allows drivers to rate customers, and (3) that mimetic pressures help explain resemblances between Finnish apps and Uber regarding ride requesting, real-time location information, and customers rating drivers.

We contribute to the IT and institutionalization research stream by illustrating how mobile applications as IT artefacts can be seen as carriers of institutional pressures that materialize in the features they provide.

This study also has several limitations. First, our analysis focuses on Finland only. Second, we focus on a customer and service-perspective. Thus, we did not focus on supply-side issues or (de-)regulation in this paper (e.g., [4, 26]).

Our study opens up avenues for future research. More research is needed to support or corroborate our findings, e.g., by conducting a similar analysis in another industry where a "disruptor" entered a highly regulated market with a mobile app. From the Finnish perspective, the de-regulation of the taxi market in July 2018 can be seen as a case of re-creation of an institution [27]. This provides interesting research opportunities: will future Finnish taxi hailing apps show more signs of mimetic pressure, with Finnish taxi apps starting to resemble more and more Uber-type applications (e.g., by incorporating surge pricing)? Will we still see signs of normative pressures where taxi apps contain values currently held by the taxi driver profession overall? We call for further empirical research on and theorization of changes in the taxi industry over longer time spans (e.g., [9]), making use of historical approaches and longitudinal data.

References

1. Stone, B.: The Upstarts: How Uber, Airbnb and the Killer Companies of the New Silicon Valley are Changing the World. Bantam Press, London (2017)
2. McGregor, M., Brown, B., Glöss, M.: Disrupting the cab: Uber, ridesharing and the taxi industry. J. Peer Prod. **6** (2015)
3. Hacker, P.: UberPop, UberBlack, and the regulation of digital platforms after the Asociación Professional Elite Taxi judgment of the CJEU. Eur. Rev. Contract Law **14**, 80–96 (2018)
4. Tucker, E.: Uber and the unmaking and remaking of taxi capitalisms: technology, law and resistance in historical perspective. In: McKee, D., Makela, F., Scassa, T. (eds.) Law and the "Sharing Economy": Regulating Online Market Platforms. University of Ottawa Press, Ottawa (2018)
5. Cramer, J., Krueger, A.B.: Disruptive change in the taxi business: the case of Uber. Am. Econ. Rev. **106**, 177–182 (2016)
6. Um, S., Yoo, Y., Berente, N., Lyytinen, K.: Digital artifacts as institutional attractors: a systems biology perspective on change in organizational routines. In: Bhattacherjee, A., Fitzgerald, B. (eds.) Shaping the Future of ICT Research. Methods and Approaches. IFIP Advances in Information and Communication Technology, vol. 389, pp. 195–209. Springer, Heidelberg (2012). https://doi.org/10.1007/978-3-642-35142-6_13
7. Boxenbaum, E., Jonsson, S.: Isomorphism, diffusion and decoupling: concept evolution and theoretical challenges. In: Greenwood, R., Oliver, C., Lawrence, T.B., Meyer, R.E. (eds.) The SAGE Handbook of Organizational Institutionalism, pp. 78–98. Sage, London (2008)
8. Gosain, S.: Enterprise information systems as objects and carriers of institutional forces: the new iron cage? J. Assoc. Inf. Syst. **5**, 6 (2004)
9. Rajão, R., Hayes, N.: Conceptions of control and IT artefacts: an institutional account of the Amazon rainforest monitoring system. J. Inf. Technol. **24**, 320–331 (2009)
10. Orlikowski, W.J., Iacono, C.S.: Research commentary: desperately seeking the "IT" in IT research—a call to theorizing the IT artifact. Inf. Syst. Res. **12**, 121–134 (2001)
11. Bekken, J.-T.: Experiences with (De-) Regulation in the European Taxi Industry. Organisation for Economic Co-operation and Development (OECD) (2007)
12. Scott, W.R.: Institutions and Organization: Ideas, Interests, and Identities. Sage, Thousand Oaks (2014)
13. DiMaggio, P., Powell, W.W.: The iron cage revisited: collective rationality and institutional isomorphism in organizational fields. Am. Sociol. Rev. **48**, 147–160 (1983)
14. Strang, D., Soule, S.A.: Diffusion in organizations and social movements: from hybrid corn to poison pills. Annu. Rev. Sociol. **24**, 265–290 (1998)

15. Mignerat, M., Rivard, S.: Positioning the institutional perspective in information systems research. J. Inf. Technol. **24**, 369–391 (2009)
16. Hasselbladh, H., Kallinikos, J.: The project of rationalization: a critique and reappraisal of neo-institutionalism in organization studies. Organ. Stud. **21**, 697–720 (2000)
17. Yin, R.K.: Case Study Research: Design and Methods. Sage Publications, Thousand Oaks, California (2009)
18. Mauranen, T.: Taksi! Matka suomalaisen taksin historiaan. Suomen taksiliitto ry, Forssa (1995)
19. Hodges, G.R.G.: Taxi! A Social History of the New York City Cabdriver. The Johns Hopkins University Press, Baltimore (2007)
20. Rayle, L., Dai, D., Chan, N., Cervero, R., Shaheen, S.: Just a better taxi? A survey-based comparison of taxis, transit, and ridesourcing services in San Francisco. Transp. Policy **45**, 168–178 (2016)
21. Crittenden, A.B., Crittenden, V.L., Crittenden, W.F.: Industry transformation via channel disruption. J. Market. Channels **24**, 13–26 (2017)
22. Zorn, T.E., Flanagin, A.J., Shoham, M.D.: Institutional and noninstitutional influences on information and communication technology adoption and use among nonprofit organizations. Hum. Commun. Res. **37**, 1–33 (2011)
23. Magnier-Watanabe, R.: An institutional perspective of mobile payment adoption: the case of Japan. In: 47th Hawaii International Conference on System Sciences (HICSS), pp. 1043–1052 (2014)
24. Lai, K.-H., Wong, C.W.Y., Cheng, T.C.E.: Institutional isomorphism and the adoption of information technology for supply chain management. Comput. Ind. **57**, 93–98 (2006)
25. David, P.A.: Why are institutions the 'carriers of history'?: Path dependence and the evolution of conventions, organizations and institutions. Struct. Change Econ. Dynam. **5**, 205–220 (1994)
26. Frizell, S.: A Historical Argument Against Uber: Taxi Regulations Are There for a Reason. Time.com N.PAG (2014)
27. Lawrence, T.B., Suddaby, R., Leca, B. (eds.): Institutional Work: Actors and Agency in Institutional Studies of Organizations. Cambridge University Press, Cambridge (2009)

Author Index

Printed in the United States
By Bookmasters